"I devoured Neil Miller's *What if Listening to* [   ]
fun, and easy to read, and it is filled with stor
From Genesis to Revelation, the Bible is full of
voice, seeing visions, receiving and interpreting dreams, and releasing the
power of God. Neil describes how all this is available today, and how these
divine encounters work transforming wonders in people's lives in South Asia.
Though we are not all called to be missionaries as Neil is, we are all called to
make disciples. Neil has given us practical insights into how we can be more
effective in this high calling. I strongly encourage you to learn from him."

—MARK VIRKLER
Founder, Communion with God Ministries; President,
Christian Leadership University; and author of *4 Keys to Hearing God's Voice*

"*What if Listening to God Was Easy?* is a well-written, biblically based, won-
derfully illustrated, and profoundly important book. Neil Miller has provided
a resource that will inspire, instruct, and engage even the most casual readers,
and as a result, position them for a life-changing encounter with God."

—TERRY WARDLE
President, Healing Care Ministries, and author of *Some Kind of Crazy:
An Unforgettable Story of Profound Brokenness and Breathtaking Grace*

"Having been raised in an evangelical world in which prayer was mostly
about talking to God and expressing my thoughts to him, it is delightful
to have a book filled with examples of people who have learned to take as
much interest and time in listening to God speak. Neil Miller weaves together
Scripture, story, and theology in ways that are easy to read but profoundly in-
sightful. I have been in rooms full of leaders who profess to know and follow
Jesus, but who, unhappily, have relied almost entirely on their own wisdom
to solve problems and make decisions rather than saying, 'Let's ask Jesus what
he thinks on the matter.' Yes, it can be that easy!"

—CHARLES DAVIS
former International Director, The Evangelical Alliance Mission (TEAM),
and author of *Making Disciples across Cultures*

"An honest book, wrapped in Scripture, and hard to put down. It is inspiring
to read example after example of lives being changed by learning to listen to
Jesus. The how-to format Neil lays out is easy to follow and easy to replicate

to others. This book will change how you listen to Jesus, thus changing how you encounter him. I am convinced, as Neil writes, 'that the missing piece is an ongoing, live meeting with Jesus.' You will be convinced of this too by the time you are done reading this book."

—MURRAY DUECK
Director, Samuel's Mantle Training Society, and author of *The Dreams We Dream: Learning to Live in the Wonder of God's Night Language*

"This book reads like a love letter to the church—an engaging and winsome invitation to sit at the feet of Jesus and to hear him tell us we have 'chosen what is better, and it will not be taken away.' This book is a gift to the church— for those of us who long for greater intimacy with God and want to declare again and again, 'You are the God who sees me.' This book is a call to the church—to move our worship beyond mere knowledge about God to a dynamic knowing of God 'in spirit and truth.' Drawing upon extensive biblical study, persistent personal devotion, and fascinating cross-cultural ministry experiences, this book is sure to help every pilgrim in the journey of faith to grow in their discernment of God's loving voice."

—HYON KIM
Global Director for People Development, SIM International

"Like Neil Miller, I am a missionary kid, and I love reading missionary stories. But this book in particular captured my attention. I have been practicing listening prayer for over twenty years, and in my ministry, I never tire of hearing God stories that result from inner-healing prayer sessions. A life transformed is the greatest testimony to God's work in a person's life. I applaud the author's courage to put into writing what may seem controversial in some contexts and cultures. His instructions are thorough and balanced and clearly give limits to what he has been trained and called to do. Although he gives plenty of sound reasoning, along with personal anecdotes and scriptural references, the true power of his words is in the application. Try it!"

—KAREN KEEGAN
Executive Director, M&K Ministry, and author of *Diamond Fractal: A Story of a Shattered Mind Made Whole*

What if Listening to God Was Easy?

What if Listening to God Was Easy?

Drawing Near to Jesus by Hearing His Voice

Neil Miller

Foreword by David Sherbino

Afterword by Mark Virkler

RESOURCE *Publications* · Eugene, Oregon

Resource Publications

An Imprint of Wipf and Stock Publishers

199 W. 8th Ave., Suite 3

Eugene, OR 97401

www.wipfandstock.com

PAPERBACK ISBN: 978-1-6667-1454-8

HARDCOVER ISBN: 978-1-6667-1455-5

EBOOK ISBN: 978-1-6667-1456-2

AUGUST 27, 2021

All Scripture quotations, unless otherwise indicated, are taken from the Holy Bible, New International Version®, NIV®. Copyright ©1973, 1978, 1984, 2011 by Biblica, Inc.™ Used by permission of Zondervan. All rights reserved worldwide. www.zondervan.com The "NIV" and "New International Version" are trademarks registered in the United States Patent and Trademark Office by Biblica, Inc.™

All Scripture quotations marked (KJV) are taken from the King James Version. Public Domain.

For confidentiality reasons, the names of many of the individuals mentioned have been changed.

Stream drawing in chapter 2 courtesy of Jacob Thomas.

Human outline in chapter 6 courtesy of https://openclipart.org/detail/314198/man-body-silhouette. Creative Commons 1.0, public domain.

Human brain in chapter 6 courtesy of https://publicdomainvectors.org/en/free-clipart/Vector-image-of-a-human-brain/34828.html. Creative Commons 1.0, public domain.

This book is dedicated to all those who gave me permission to use their stories and to the readers who take the subject of listening to God to heart.

Contents

Foreword by David Sherbino | ix

INTRODUCTION | 1

CHAPTER 1   Are We Missing Something? | 7

CHAPTER 2   A Simple Method of Listening to Jesus | 16

CHAPTER 3   Does God Speak Through Dreams? | 29

CHAPTER 4   Seeing Visions | 43

CHAPTER 5   Mistakes and Discernment | 54

CHAPTER 6   Understanding the Spiritual Realm | 66

CHAPTER 7   Listening in Discipleship | 78

CHAPTER 8   Listening and Inner Healing | 90

CHAPTER 9   Listening in Outreach | 103

CONCLUSION   Why This Probably Won't Work for You | 115

Afterword: The Church Owes the World an Encounter With God
        by Mark Virkler | 119

APPENDIX 1   Resources for Further Study | 123

APPENDIX 2   Answering Common Objections | 127

APPENDIX 3   Some Thoughts on Interpreting the Bible | 131

Acknowledgments | 137

BIBLIOGRAPHY | 139

Foreword

GOD CREATED US TO be in a relationship with him. This implies we ought to be able to hear his voice as he speaks to us. Jesus said, "My sheep listen to my voice; I know them, and they follow me" (John 10:27). Is it possible to hear the voice of God?

Neil Miller has written an intriguing book developed out of ministry experiences in South Asia, entitled *What if Listening to God Was Easy?* Many assume God speaks to us primarily through Scripture. Neil, however, pushes the reader to think about other ways God might be speaking. Does he speak through our thoughts? Through our dreams or visions? What is the place of the imagination and how does God use that to reveal himself? Does God even speak to unbelievers? These questions are challenging but Neil helps the reader explore these issues in a manner that is engaging, supported by Scripture, and illustrated by personal stories.

Neil acknowledges that learning to hear the voice of God has been challenging and at times he has not correctly discerned what God was saying. However, he provides the readers with insights that will help them avoid the same errors.

As you read, you will hear Neil's passion to help people discover and develop intimacy with God. He will show you practical steps that will enable you to develop an ongoing conversation with God which will enrich your life.

I recommend that you read and learn. This book, if taken seriously, will change your life and ministry.

David Sherbino
Author of *Reconnect: Spiritual Exercises to Develop Intimacy With God*
Professor of Spirituality and Pastoral Ministry
Tyndale Seminary, TORONTO, CANADA

Introduction

Jesus Raised His Right Hand

When Rashid phoned and asked to see me, I knew the situation would be difficult. With a phenomenal track record of leading people to faith in Christ, he had been one of the most successful outreach workers to partner with our organization's ministry. That had fallen apart four years ago when he was accused of romantically pursuing the wife of a colleague. As a result, Rashid lost his job. All attempts to help him start a secular business had failed miserably. Now Rashid's wife and children were living with her parents, the children were no longer in school, and Rashid himself was living off the kindness of a Muslim relative. Rashid made repeated calls to our teammates, requesting a financial bailout. His requests left us feeling guilty, but simply giving him money didn't seem like the right solution either.

Rashid was coming to see me in my office, and I was not looking forward to a long conversation full of tearful pleadings for monetary assistance. The day was full, and I fit Rashid in between several other people who had come to see me that day. I listened to him for a while and then suggested we pray. In the middle of my prayer, I stopped. Rashid's head was still bowed. I asked him to picture himself in a peaceful place. Then, in that peaceful place, I asked him to look for Jesus. "Where is Jesus?" I asked. When he could see Jesus, I asked a few more questions. "How is he relating to you? Is he coming toward you or moving away? What is the emotion on his face? Is he happy? Angry?"

Then I waited. When he looked up, I asked him what he experienced. Rashid replied, "I saw him lift up his right hand and say, 'I have never left you.'" Rashid's tears were beginning to flow, so I got up and found the tissue box. Rashid continued, "It is true. He has never left me." That five-minute experience during a busy day deeply touched Rashid's heart. He thanked me profusely and said several times, "I will never forget this as long as I live."

As I thought about this some time later, I was curious what the gesture of raising one's right hand meant. A bit of research showed me that this is a sign of taking an oath. Indeed, the Lord himself raised his hand when he swore to Abraham to give him land as a possession. (See Exod 6:8 and Ezek 20:5.) In the strongest language possible, Jesus was saying that he had never left Rashid and that he would take care of him.

Since Rashid lives in another city, we were not in regular contact. When we talked on the phone a year later, he told me that his family was living together again, all his children were in school, and he had a part-time job with another organization. This brief experience of hearing Jesus's voice profoundly impacted Rashid.

Why Write This Book?

Over the past three years, I have led numerous people into experiences of listening to Jesus. I have done this with foreign missionary workers in English and with local citizens in their heart language. I have done this with individuals and in groups. I have even experimented with leading Muslims in listening sessions. My conclusion is that this last three-year period has been the most significant and effective of my entire twenty years of ministry in South Asia.

More importantly, everything I have been doing is completely transferable to the ordinary Christian who loves Jesus and wants to obey him, whether living on the mission field or living in one's home country. Although I am open to the charismatic gifts, I don't believe that we need any special spiritual anointing to listen to Jesus. It is simply a matter of having a little bit of faith and learning how Jesus speaks.

My goals in putting my experiences in book form are threefold. First, I want to help people to know Jesus in a deeper way. The primary way that people get to know each other is through conversation. If we learn to have daily conversations with Jesus, not only will we get to know Jesus better, but our own lives will be transformed. Jesus will begin to speak into deep issues in our hearts. He will loose us from emotional chains that bind us. He will show us how to process difficult experiences. He will guide our lives.

My second goal in writing this book is to lead my readers to greater effectiveness in ministry. Jesus was effective in ministry because he listened to his Father's instructions and obeyed them. Paul and his team planted many churches, as described in the book of Acts, because they heard what the Holy Spirit was saying to them. We will become more effective in ministry if we learn to listen to Jesus and obey what he tells us.

My third goal in writing this book is to advance the Great Commission by giving people a non-threatening tool that they can use to reach out to their non-Christian friends and neighbors. Non-Christians hear God's voice too, and we can lead them in experiences of listening to Jesus.

The Context that Birthed This Book

Most of the events in this book took place in South Asia, a region stretching from Afghanistan in the northwest to Sri Lanka in the southeast. This vast region, with a population of almost two billion people, is home to Muslims, Hindus, and Buddhists. Only 2 percent of the people in this region would identify themselves as Christian.[1] While the thoughts in this book come out of the crucible of ministry in South Asia, the concepts are applicable to any ministry situation and to any person who seeks to follow Jesus in a real and practical way.

As people listen to Jesus and obey, their character and attitudes change, and these changes begin to impact those around them. Others are changed through them. If every Christian learned how to listen to Jesus on a daily basis, if they learned that they could come to him at any time and bring any matter that they were concerned about to him and hear his answers, if they learned to obey what Jesus told them, then the world would be transformed within a few generations.

I hope that this book will help to create an army of disciples—men and women who hear Jesus's voice and obey and who, in turn, teach others to listen and obey. It is my prayer that through reading this book, you will become part of this army whose commander-in-chief is the Lord Jesus. May the reading of this book result in your life being transformed and in others being transformed through you.

---

1. See https://en.wikipedia.org/wiki/South_Asia for an overview of South Asia, including the religious breakdown. For a different definition of South Asia and with a slightly lower estimate of the number of Christians see https://joshuaproject.net/regions/4.

The Importance of Stories

I like stories, and I believe stories are one of the most powerful teaching tools available. Except for chapter 6, each chapter contains stories—true events—where people listened to Jesus. While some names and minor details have been changed to protect the privacy of those involved, these are actual events, not fictional composites of several people. The conversation dialogues were written either during the listening session or shortly after.

I share these stories with some reluctance. When someone relates an event where God has worked, both the speaker and the listener tend to consider the speaker to be someone special. This is not the case. You can do everything I have done in this book too, regardless of your level of spiritual giftedness or spiritual maturity.

ReadMe.1st

When I pick up a book, I like to read it from cover to cover. Others like to jump around in a book, and still others will only read the chapters that are relevant to them. While I think you will get the most out of the book if you read the whole thing, the chapters are written so that they can stand alone. This book is for you. Feel free to read it in a way that is most beneficial to you.

In the early days of personal computers, software almost always came with a ReadMe.1st file, giving important usage instructions. For those not inclined to read a book from cover to cover, here is some ReadMe.1st information to allow you to choose what parts you want to read:

- **Chapter 1: Are We Missing Something?** In this chapter, I survey how God spoke to people in the Bible, interspersing these accounts with real-life examples.

- **Chapter 2: A Simple Method of Listening to Jesus.** I have read many books on listening to God, but few give a simple process we can use to know how to hear God's voice. In this chapter, I provide a simple method many people have found helpful as they start on their journey of listening to Jesus.

- **Chapter 3: Does God Speak Through Dreams?** People through the ages have looked to dreams for guidance. What does the Bible say about this? Are there principles we can apply to interpret our dreams?

- **Chapter 4: Seeing Visions.** Visions are a common way God speaks, but most of the time, we discount the visions God gives us. This chapter shows how we can learn to see visions.

- **Chapter 5: Mistakes and Discernment.** Sometimes we make mistakes in listening. Why do we not always hear God correctly? In this chapter, I show how we can learn to distinguish God's voice from the other voices we hear.

- **Chapter 6: Understanding the Spiritual Realm.** This chapter is for those who really like to understand how things work. I explain how the spiritual and physical realms intersect with each other.

- **Chapter 7: Listening in Discipleship.** Here, I present listening to Jesus as a discipleship skill that can and should be taught in discipling relationships.

- **Chapter 8: Listening and Inner Healing.** Almost all of us have experienced hurts in our journey through life. Jesus's voice brings deep healing for these hurts.

- **Chapter 9: Listening in Outreach.** After experimenting with leading non-Christians in listening to God, I conclude that listening sessions can be used to introduce others to the God whom we love.

For those who want to go deeper, at the end of the book, I have included an annotated bibliography of helpful books and resources. This is followed by an appendix looking at some common objections to the idea of hearing God's voice. The last appendix explores how the way we interpret the Bible affects our openness to hearing God's voice.

I Feel Very Happy

It was another busy day in the office. We were interviewing candidates for a job opening, and lots of people were in and out of the office in addition to those on the interview board. Fazil, a very faithful believer whom I have come to love, also wanted to spend some time with me. He had things on his mind and just wanted time to pray with me.

When I had a free moment, we sat down together. Perhaps in part due to the rash of busy thoughts swirling around in my own mind, I felt the need to start by quieting our hearts and listening to Jesus. I told Fazil to see himself in a quiet, peaceful place. He was also busy that day and took several minutes to settle on a place in his mind. Finally, he saw himself on the flat concrete roof of his village home—often a person can go to be alone on the rooftop. He saw himself bowed down at Jesus's feet. As he waited, Fazil saw the Lord lift him up and embrace him. Evidently, Jesus wanted to see Fazil in the position of a friend and brother, not in the position of a slave. After it was over, Fazil's eyes were moist with tears, but they were happy tears. When Fazil left, I realized I hadn't even prayed for him. All I did was lead him to Jesus. That was enough.

Chapter 1

Are We Missing Something?

Kristen's Story

KRISTEN, A WOMAN WITH a passion for the Lord and our first team member in South Asia from a nearby East Asian country, stopped over one Saturday afternoon to visit my wife, Ingrid. Since Kristen came early and Ingrid was not free to meet with her just then, I decided to break out of my introverted shell, be polite, and try to talk to her. Our conversation went something like this:

Kristen:	What do you think? Should we as foreigners be involved in outreach? Shouldn't we rather disciple the local people and let them reach out with the good news?
Neil:	I think we should be involved in both. It doesn't make sense for us to try to encourage local people to do something we are not doing ourselves.
Kristen:	So how do you go about the process of reaching out to your neighbors?
Neil:	I look for opportunities to pray with people. For example, if someone is sick, I ask if I can pray for them.
Kristen:	Does God still do miracles of healing today? I've been taught he does not heal anymore.

We followed this with a time of looking at some passages of Scripture, focusing particularly on what Jesus taught his disciples to do. After a while,

I got an uncomfortable feeling in the pit of my stomach. "Neil, ask her if there is any sickness in her body." At this point in my journey, I was neither skilled nor confident in praying for healing. I was afraid that if I prayed for her and nothing happened, she would become entrenched in her position that God no longer heals people today as she had been taught. However, I followed the prompting of the Holy Spirit. Our conversation continued as follows:

Neil: Do you have any sickness in your body?

Kristen: Yes.

Neil: Do you feel comfortable sharing what it is?

Kristen: No.

Neil: That is not a problem. Let's pray.

So I began to pray. In the middle of my prayer, I asked Kristen to think about the biblical event where a sick woman pressed through the crowd and touched Jesus's clothes (Luke 8:43–48). I told Kristen to picture the scene. There were crowds of people, noise, and Jesus in the center. Then I asked her to picture herself pressing through the crowd with the desire to touch Jesus's clothes.

Then I waited. My eyes were open. Kristen's were closed, and her head was bowed. The waiting time is hard because I have no idea what is going on in the heart of the person I am praying with. Was she just showing Eastern politeness and waiting for me to continue? Or was something going on in her heart? When I saw a tear roll down Kristen's cheek, I knew that God was working in her heart.

When Kristen opened her eyes, I asked her what had happened. She replied, "I didn't want to touch Jesus's clothes. I wanted to go right up to him and hold on to his feet. As I knelt there, bowed at his feet, he touched my head and said to me, 'I have completely healed you. Go and preach the gospel.'" Later, Kristen explained to me that the person who shared the gospel with her had experienced a physical healing. After that, Kristen had been taught that God does not do miracles of healing today.

Does God Still Speak?

What should we make of Kristen's story? Does God still do miracles? Does God speak to people in a conversational manner? Can we easily learn how to listen to him? Like Kristen, many people have been taught that God no longer works in the same way that he worked in the Bible. We read about the many miracles in the Bible. We believe they occurred because of our belief in the inspiration of Scripture, but we don't expect to experience similar encounters today. Sometimes, like Gideon, we long to see something miraculous.

"'But sir,' Gideon replied, 'if the Lord is with us, why has all this happened to us? Where are all his wonders that our fathers told us about when they said, "Did not the Lord bring us up out of Egypt?" But now the Lord has abandoned us and put us into the hand of Midian'" (Judg 6:13).

Most of the time, however, we consign ourselves to a reality where God feels distant and does not regularly or discernably interact with us. After all, we are taught that the miracles were given to establish the church. Now that the church has been established, we no longer need miracles. We just need to accept what we are taught by faith and try to live our lives as best we can.

But is that what God intends for us? Let's survey how God communicated with people in the Bible. Let's look at some real-life examples. Finally, let's draw our own conclusions.

An angry man

We expect that Adam and Eve had a conversational relationship with God. After all, they were in Eden; there was no sin. When they were banished from God's presence, we would expect that God's conversation with people ceased. But did it? Cain, Adam and Eve's firstborn, was full of murderous anger. Clearly not in a right relationship with God, Cain was most certainly not the epitome of a fine, upstanding Christian. What happened? God spoke to him and warned him about his anger and showed him the path to being accepted (Gen 4:4–7).

Real-life example

Our organization was having its annual Christmas party, but Greg was in no mood to celebrate. He had been deeply offended by another colleague's disparaging comments. Greg and I sat together, quieted our hearts, and listened to Jesus. As Greg listened, he realized that the way Jesus saw him was totally different from the way his colleague saw him. The anger and pain melted away.

A runaway woman

Noah and Abraham are heroes of the faith. We set them on a pedestal and don't doubt that God would talk to them. When we look at our own lives with our grumpy moods, rebellious attitudes, and sometimes outright disobedience, we do not expect God to talk to us. We wouldn't normally consider Hagar to be one of our heroes—she is a bit too much like us in her response to problems. She was not a prophetess but a slave. And there is evidence she had some serious, unhealed emotional issues. When circumstances became difficult, largely because of her own disrespectful behavior, she ran away from her problems. In that situation, not only did God communicate with her through an angel, but God gave her a powerful blessing (Gen 16:1–10).

Real-life example

Kalpona struggled to get along with her roommates. She compared herself to others around her who had great upbringings while she faced so much suffering in life. It wasn't fair. Where was God? When we met to pray together, she felt as if she had no hope. But God spoke to her during our prayer time. At the end of the session, there was a marked difference in her emotional outlook. She said, "Thanks. I've never done this kind of prayer with anyone before. I didn't even know these things were hurting me."

A pagan king

Then there was Abimelech, the Philistine king who was not even part of the covenant people of God. He made an innocent mistake based on false information Abraham had given him. What did God do? God communicated with him and told him of the error he had made and the consequences that would occur if he did not make it right (Gen 20:1–7).

Real-life example

I have known Mr. Khaled, an elderly Muslim man, for about seventeen years. He has come to church a few times, and during several visits in our home, we have prayed together. During one visit, he told me he would pray and meditate on God daily. On the next visit, I asked how that had been going. His answer told me this had not been going so well. But then he asked, "Can we do it now?" With Muslims, I never know whether to do a meditation focused on Jesus, whom they regard as merely a prophet, or on God the Father. Since he had initiated the request, I decided I would be bold and lead him in a meditation on Jesus. When it was over, he told me what he experienced. He said, "I saw him. He touched me. He embraced me."

A new leader

Moses had a deep conversational relationship with God. We'll meet him later in this book, so we'll skip over him now. But what about Joshua, his protégé? After Joshua and his army spectacularly defeated Jericho, Joshua relied on the wisdom of his scouts to make his next strategic move. He decided that the whole army was not required to defeat Ai, and he did not stop to ask the Lord his thoughts on the matter. That decision resulted in disastrous defeat (Josh 7:1–6).

After listening to God's reason for the rout at Ai and correcting the problem, Joshua and his army engaged in a number of successful military campaigns until they met the Gibeonites. The Gibeonites, realizing they didn't stand a chance against Joshua, resorted to a ruse. They claimed to be from a distant country and asked Joshua to make a peace treaty with them, sworn in the name of the Lord. The biblical text clearly states the omission. "The Israelites sampled their provisions but did not inquire of the Lord" (Josh 9:14). God expected Joshua to check in with him when he was not certain about what to do. When Joshua skipped that step, he made mistakes.

Real-life example

Extremists were getting bolder and were targeting minorities in our location. Islamic State was taking credit for these attacks. Every month it seemed, the newspaper reported another attack or targeted killing—a

Hindu priest, a Buddhist monk, an atheist blogger, a foreign aid worker, or a Christian pastor.

As the country director of an organization with more than fifty, mostly White, foreign adults, I knew we were highly visible and a relatively easy target. I didn't want to encourage our people to pull up and leave as some other organizations were doing, but at the same time, I didn't want to make a stupid leadership decision that would result in one of my colleagues being killed. As I paced and prayed on my office veranda one day, a thought popped into my mind. *Pray that none of your people are killed.* I began to pray that prayer daily, and none of our team members were harmed.

David's battle strategies

David and his valiant band of fighting men were on the run from King Saul. When they saw that the city of Keilah was being attacked by the Philistines, David wondered if he should fight off the invaders. He asked God, and God told him to go ahead. His men were not so sure and responded, "Here in Judah we are afraid. How much more, then, if we go to Keilah against the Philistine forces!" (1 Sam 23:3). So David asked God again, and God gave the same answer. David then successfully defeated the Philistines and entered the city. Saul, learning David was inside a walled city, thought David would now be easy prey. Upon hearing that Saul was on his way, David needed to know if the citizens of Keilah would protect him or hand him over to Saul. The Lord told David that Saul would come and the citizens of Keilah would not protect him. In the first twelve verses of 1 Sam 23, God speaks to David four times.

David firmly believed that God communicates, and this belief is reflected in many of the Psalms. The following psalm, although not explicitly attributed to David, expresses this belief.

> But their idols are silver and gold,
>   made by human hands.
> They have mouths, but cannot speak,
>   eyes, but cannot see.
> They have ears, but cannot hear,
>   noses, but they cannot smell.
> They have hands, but cannot feel,
>   feet, but they cannot walk,
>   nor can they utter a sound with their throats (Ps 115:4–7).

The point is, God is not like a deaf, mute, lifeless idol. God speaks.

God's Voice in the New Testament

The biblical record is clear. God spoke frequently to people in the Old Testament. But maybe God doesn't work the same way he did in the past. Did he change the way he communicates in the New Testament? God's communication is different in the New Testament—it's more accessible. When Peter stood up to preach after the pouring out of the Holy Spirit at Pentecost, he made it clear that the Holy Spirit is for everyone: women and men, old and young. And when the Holy Spirit comes, he communicates. This communication comes in the form of prophecy, visions, dreams, and signs (Acts 2:17–19).

Now, we all have access to the Holy Spirit. We can all hear God's voice. Paul continues this theme when he talks about spiritual gifts. He says, "You know that when you were pagans, somehow or other you were influenced and led astray to mute idols" (1 Cor 12:2). He draws the same conclusion as the psalmist before him: idols are mute, but our God speaks. The New Testament examples of God's communication are abundant. God spoke through signs (Acts 4:31), words of knowledge (Acts 5:3), angelic appearances (Acts 8:26), visions (Acts 9:3–6, 10–16), direct communication by the Holy Spirit (Acts 13:2), and direct appearances of the Lord (Acts 23:11). Most of the book of Revelation is an extended visionary experience, revealing things to come in symbolic language.

Some Conclusions

As we look at the biblical data from Genesis to Revelation, we see example after example of God speaking to people. We see godly people who hear his voice. And we see others who are not so godly: Cain in his anger, Hagar in her rebellion, and Abimelech outside the covenant. In the New Testament, after Christ's death, resurrection, and ascension, we see the same thing. God continues to speak. In fact, the coming of the Holy Spirit means an increase in hearing God's voice. God's voice is for all people. The Bible never gives any indication that God's speaking relationship with people is supposed to stop.

How Does Listening to God Relate to the Gospel?

Paul makes it clear that the gospel is of primary importance. The gospel or "good news" is the message that Jesus died for our sins, that he was buried, and that he was raised on the third day. This good news is so important that without it, our faith is completely futile. If this message is not true, then we are to be pitied more than all people (1 Cor 15:19).

So what does hearing God's voice have to do with the gospel? Might it be a distraction from our main message that we are forgiven from sin through Jesus and that we need to repent? Shouldn't we rather focus on preaching the gospel and not trouble ourselves with the whole idea of listening to God?

Let's step back a minute and think about what the gospel brings about. Jesus, through his death and resurrection, brings us into reconciliation with God (Rom 5:11; 2 Cor 5:18). Reconciliation means "restoration to divine favor"[1] or, in colloquial terms, "the act of causing two people or groups to become friendly again after an argument or disagreement."[2] After reconciliation happens, the two parties can have fellowship. Indeed, fellowship with God is assumed to be the normal state for the Christian (1 John 1:6). Here's the key point: fellowship requires communication. It is impossible to have fellowship with another person without communicating.

Let's look at this idea from another vantage point. One of the names given to Jesus prior to his birth was "Immanuel" which means "God with us" (Matt 1:23). Then, shortly before his ascension to heaven, Jesus said, "I am with you always" (Matt 28:20). It makes little sense to think of being constantly with another person without having regular communication. Jesus made the expectation of communication explicit when he talked to his disciples about the coming Holy Spirit. One of the things the Holy Spirit does is speak (John 16:13).

Listening to God is not a distraction from the gospel but a direct outcome of the gospel. When we are reconciled to God through Jesus's death on the cross, we are brought into fellowship with God. Fellowship requires communication.

---

1. *Mickelson's*, s. v. "G2643 *katallage*."
2. *Merriam-Webster.com*, s.v. "reconciliation."

Where Does the Bible Fit in to Listening to God?

If God speaks to us directly, then what do we need the Bible for? Why don't we just do away with the Bible and focus on listening to God? Our problem is that we are not guaranteed to hear God correctly every time. God certainly speaks, but sometimes our spiritual ears are not open to his voice (Jer 6:10). Our competing desires and idols in our hearts may obscure the message God is communicating to us. For example, in Ezek 14:3–4, the elders of Israel had set up idols in their hearts, so God promised to answer them accordingly. In other words, they would face confusion when they went to inquire of the Lord because of the idols in their hearts. For these reasons, we need an objective standard—the Bible—by which to measure what we are hearing. If anything we hear is contrary to the teaching of the Bible, we must throw it out.

It is my basic assumption that we are being shaped by Scripture on a daily basis. We read it and allow the message to form us and to direct the way we lead our lives. The Bible not only shows us the way of salvation through Jesus, it helps us to understand the loving heart of God. God will never give us a message that contradicts Scripture because God does not contradict himself. Yet, the numerous biblical examples of God speaking through such means as dreams, visions, and angelic appearances demonstrate that God never intended to limit himself to only speaking through the written pages of the Bible.

In the next chapter, we will learn one way to tune in to God's voice.

Chapter 2

A Simple Method of Listening to Jesus

Jesus Took the Burden Off

DR. H AND HIS wife K are the Korean leaders of a small team seeking to establish a new work in our region. Since our organization has been established for many years, and since I was the director, they came to me for advice. In my first few years of leadership, I felt woefully inadequate to be advising anyone on anything, much less suggesting how members of another organization should work in this country. I just hoped I had survived in my role long enough that my team members wouldn't conclude that I was simply figuring things out as I went along.

The first and second times H came, we talked about which areas of the country were less reached and the different approaches to engage in ministry here. The third time, I talked about the importance of vision in leadership. By the fourth time he visited, I was less reticent about giving advice. When he contacted me about meeting again, I decided to take some time to pray and to ask if the Lord had anything to say to me about this coaching time. The Lord said, "I desire to talk to him, and his questions are the door to bring him into a conversational relationship with me."

This time, H brought his wife. The subject on their minds was the appropriateness of hiring local citizens in their particular ministry. I gave them my perspective but told them that it would be even better to seek the Lord's perspective. I suggested leading them in a time of listening to the Lord. I explained my simple procedure of quieting our hearts, fixing our eyes on Jesus, asking him a question, and noting the answer. I could see

16

that they were eagerly following what I had to say and were willing to give this process a try.

During our listening session, K related what was going on in her heart, and I scribbled down notes as fast as I could write. After the listening time, we talked more about what she had heard. As K shared, she began to cry. Her tears of joy indicated that this listening session touched on something much deeper than questions about whom to hire. Jesus beautifully addressed an issue hidden in her heart. K had been feeling the pressure of leadership, particularly the need to do things right because their actions would be a critical determinant of their team's ministry culture. As she described her encounter with Jesus, she said, "It was like he just took the burden off." God spoke to H too. Even though for him, the message was not accompanied by the same level of emotion, it was also significant. Jesus was telling him not to stress out so much in his position as leader.

Listening to God Is Easy

Listening to God is easy. God is a loving father. Fathers talk to their children. God wants to talk to us. He is willing to engage with us on any subject we bring to him. He will talk to us any time we choose to listen. He is probably hurt when we don't feel the need to ask him our questions, and we think the wisest thing to do is to figure things out on our own the best we can. Our main problem is not that God doesn't speak but that we don't know how to listen and that we are too full of doubt.

Tuning In to Flowing Thoughts

So what does God's voice sound like? Mark Virkler explains, "His voice sounds like spontaneous thoughts that light upon your mind, especially as your heart is fixed on Him."[1]

Jesus likened God's Spirit to a stream. (See John 7:37–39.) A stream constantly flows. We, therefore, need to think in terms of flowing thoughts when we are seeking to tune in to what the Holy Spirit is saying. When I introduce others to the idea of listening to Jesus, I often sketch a little picture. I include several objects in my sketch: a stream, fixed objects on the bank of the stream, an object floating in the stream, and the listener on the bank.

1. Virkler, 4 Keys, 13.

The trees and rocks represent our own thoughts, our fixed ways of thinking that do not easily change. Our own thoughts may be good or bad, but they have been there, established in our minds, for years. God's voice usually comes to us as flowing thoughts.[2] These thoughts are new and fresh and help us see the situation differently. If you are sitting on the bank of a stream and see a toy sailboat floating by, you had better grab it quickly; otherwise, it will float away before you realize it. Likewise, when we ask God a question and he puts a flowing thought in our hearts, we must grab on to that thought immediately; otherwise, we will lose it.

This leads us to one of the primary problems in listening experiences. We quiet our hearts. We fix our eyes on Jesus. We ask him a question. And Jesus responds to our entreaty. He answers. He puts a thought in the Holy Spirit's flowing stream. But we ignore it. We sense a tiny little thought flowing in the back of our mind, but we dismiss it because (a) it seems irrelevant, (b) it seems unimportant, (c) we don't understand it, or (d) we doubt that this is a thought from God. And so, the moment is gone. We must learn to grab these flowing thoughts before they disappear.

2. Virkler, *4 Keys*, 24–25.

How Can We Listen?

God speaks in many different ways. We cannot limit him to one particular procedure. However, many people find it helpful, especially in the beginning, to follow a simple procedure. As a person grows in his listening experience, he no longer needs to rely on a procedure. In the following section, I explain a simple procedure that many people have found helpful.

- Quiet your soul and your body
- Fix your eyes on Jesus
- Ask Jesus a question
- Verbalize the answer
- Test it later

Quiet Your Soul and Your Body

For most of our lives, our soul is focused on what is going on in our body and therefore is not aware of what is going on in our spirit. If we want to tune in to what is happening in our spirit (the place where God speaks to us), our soul and body need to come to a place of stillness. Sitting comfortably in a quiet place with your eyes closed will help reduce the input from your physical surroundings. I usually tell people to take several deep breaths. New age groups seem to have cornered the market on deep breathing, but it does not need to be this way. In fact, several scientific studies show that the relaxation response can be achieved simply by breathing deeply for a few minutes.[3] When our minds and bodies have quieted down, we can move on to the next step.

Fix Your Eyes on Jesus

We can fix our eyes on Jesus in several ways. It is almost always best to start by entering a positive mental picture or memory. Often, when a person begins to listen to Jesus, she feels tense, either about the subject she wants to ask Jesus or about whether she will be able to hear what Jesus is saying. If intense emotions make it difficult to communicate with people whom we

3. Kozub, "Take a Deep Breath." See also Martin, "Relaxation Response," 32.

can see, how much more will such emotions hinder our communication with Jesus whom we cannot see? Directing our minds to a positive picture causes us to feel God's love and open ourselves up to his communication. Here are some ways we can do this.

Method 1: Return to a positive memory

The first way to help a person fix their eyes on Jesus is to ask the person to return to a positive memory. This could be a time where she felt especially close to God or where God powerfully helped her in a time of need or when God spoke to her in the past. When the person has such a memory in mind, I ask her to re-enter it and imagine that she is there again. When the person sees herself back in the memory, I ask her to look around and see where Jesus is.

Example: On a boat in a storm

Lilli spent much time as a child on a sailing yacht with her family. When I asked her to return in her memory to a time when God especially helped her, she saw herself as a little girl on the yacht with her family in a life-threatening storm. After the listening time was over, Lilli said, "I don't know why God brought that event to mind. It happened so long ago. In fact, I had actually forgotten it." Remembering God's care and protection for her deeply moved Lilli.

Method 2: Return to a pleasant place

Another way to fix your spiritual eyes on Jesus is to use your powers of imagination to see yourself in a peaceful scene. This could be an actual physical place or a mentally created picture of a peaceful place. After the person sees himself in that pleasant place, I ask him to look around and see where Jesus is. On occasion, I have asked the person to picture someone coming to him, and that person is Jesus.

Example: Beside the water

Henry grew up in the United States and was the newly appointed leader of a mission organization. When we listened to Jesus together, Henry saw himself at a childhood swimming place out in the countryside where he grew up. He was sitting there beside the water with Jesus seated beside him with his arm around him.

Another man, Masud, grew up in a region known for its rivers. He saw himself on a wide sandbar in the middle of a large river. He saw a small boat come up to the sandbar, and a man got off the boat. That man was Jesus.

Method 3: Enter a Bible story

Another way to help a person fix her eyes on Jesus is to lead her to see herself as part of a Bible story or other passage of Scripture. Stories in the gospels are helpful for some people. Other people can see a picture described by a passage, such as a shepherd with his sheep (Ps 23), or a room with a door (Rev 3:20).

Example: In the story

Kristen saw herself as a woman pushing through the crowd to come to Jesus. (See Luke 8:43–48.) Dave saw himself in a boat with Jesus in the middle of a storm. (See Luke 8:22–25.) Tufayel saw himself inside a room. (See Rev 3:20.) He heard Jesus knocking, but a lot of weeds were covering the door. He struggled to get through the weeds and open it.

Method 4: Imagine Jesus sitting in the room with you

Yet another way to help a person tune in to Jesus is to ask her to picture Jesus right there in the room.

Example: Coronavirus fears

As we talked and prayed over WhatsApp, Sylvia told how she was experiencing anxiety over the coronavirus situation and the possible impact on her loved ones. I asked her to picture Jesus there in the room with her.

When she could see Jesus in her mind's eye, I asked her to bring her worries to Jesus in a box and watch what he did with them. Sylvia said, "Jesus is saying that he is here for me always. I don't need to worry about all these things. I should remove these from my mind forever."

Since Sylvia had been experiencing severe back pain for the past few days, I suggested that if she wanted to, she could ask Jesus to put his hand on her back. Still in the prayer experience, Sylvia exclaimed on the other end of the line, "I think Jesus just touched my muscles. I can feel something happening. I can feel some change." After the prayer time, she said, "I'm feeling much better now. I'm not feeling any pain."

A Note on Using Our Imagination

Many people have a hard time accepting the fact that God speaks to us through the thing we call imagination, but the imagination is an instrument God uses to talk to us. All our lives, most of us have believed that we create what we see in our imagination, that it's artificial or make-believe. A more helpful way to view the imagination is to see it as a theater movie screen. The pictures displayed on the screen may be what we create ourselves, what God gives us to view, or pictures from an evil source. (We will look at discernment of the source more closely in chapter 5.)

We learn to view what is happening in the spiritual realm by looking through the window of our imagination. The picture we begin with is simply a starting place. As we enter the picture and look for Jesus, the picture comes alive, and we begin to interact with Jesus.

Ask a Question

After a person has an awareness of Jesus's presence, the conversation can begin. Usually, the person's eyes are still closed and in order not to break his concentration, I ask him to simply nod to indicate a sense of Jesus's presence. When the person has a sense of Jesus's presence, I then tell him to ask a question and mentally note the answer. It is important here to note down the first thoughts that come even if they appear to be unconnected to the question.

In one of my first significant listening experiences, I was asking God why I felt as if he never answered my prayers. A childhood memory of being in a toy store with my parents floated into my mind. I tried a couple of times to dismiss this apparent distraction, but it kept returning. Finally, I figured out that God might be trying to speak to me through that memory. That memory of loss (the toy was not purchased) and the Holy Spirit's subsequent word to my heart unlocked a deep level of healing.

Good questions to ask

According to Murray Dueck, director of Samuel's Mantle Training Society, "Our understanding of what God thinks about us is the most important thing in our relationship with him."[4]

To build trust and grow in their relationship with God, I usually coach the listener to ask Jesus a question, such as, "How much do you love me?" This question works well for people who are unchurched or who have very little Bible background. When a Muslim schoolteacher asked God that question for the first time, tears immediately came to her eyes. She received the revelation that God loved her as much as she loves her own son. For people who have been in church all their lives, this question is less powerful because they know the Sunday School answer that Jesus loved them enough to go to the cross for them. For these people, a more helpful question is: "Jesus, when you look at me, what do you think of me?"

Carrying burdens

Mrs. Aktar is a heavyset woman who seems to be the one holding her family together. She came into my office one day, requesting prayer but unwilling to tell me what her burdens were. As I reflected on how to handle this request, I decided that leading her to listen to Jesus would help her the most. Since this was one of the first times I had done this with her, I had her ask Jesus what he thought of her. Jesus said, "You have the ability to carry the load. Be patient." That was the encouragement she needed, and at the end of the prayer time, she said she felt very light.

After the first question, I usually ask the person to open her eyes and tell me what is going on. The simple act of verbalizing makes the image much more powerful. For many, tears don't come until they verbalize what has happened.

---

4. Murray Dueck, personal communication with author, December 2020.

When I am assured that the person is positively interacting with the Lord, I invite her to return to that picture of being with Jesus and ask other questions that are on her heart. Here, the questions need to be specific. Sometimes the person has a swirl of thoughts in her mind, which might include a whole lot of questions. In this confused state, she does not know what her questions are and so cannot hear God's answers. The listener must narrow these down to one specific question at a time. At times, I have coached the person to actually write down the question before she asks it. If God's answer to the first question sparks another question, the listener should allow the conversation to flow. If the listener receives a thought that does not make sense, the appropriate thing to do is to ask Jesus questions about that thought.

Verbalize the Answer

The listener will not grasp the import of the answer until she verbalizes it, either to another person or, if she is doing this alone, to her journal. Putting the interaction we have with Jesus into words is very powerful. The thoughts or pictures we receive may appear unconnected or inapplicable at first. Verbalizing the answer helps us connect the dots. The very act of putting into words the thoughts we have received makes them more concrete. Dr. Karl Lehman has written extensively about the importance of sharing our listening experiences with another person.

> When we describe our mental content to a facilitator or others in a small group, the combination of the social interaction task and the language task causes the content we are describing to be processed through both our right and left prefrontal cortices and thereby enables us to feel the importance of the content we are describing, to perceive the meaning of the content we are describing, and especially to perceive how the content fits into our personal autobiographical stories.[5]

Lehman, who has spent thousands of hours leading others in listening encounters, shares the personal benefit he received from doing the same thing in his own life.

> Later in the day as I described this experience to Charlotte, intense emotions began welling up as I was telling the story, and by

5. Lehman, *Immanuel Approach*, 182.

the time I had finished I had a much clearer, keener perception of what it all meant. Until I described the experience to Charlotte, I had not been able to fully feel its importance or to fully comprehend its meaning. As I think about this now, my assessment is that I had been missing 80 to 90 percent of the blessing until I talked to Charlotte about it.[6]

When I am leading someone in the listening process, I ask him to tell me what is going on in his heart. Sometimes the answer is clear and powerful, but many times, the person does not fully understand the answer. If this is the first time, most often, the person is doubtful he has heard from the Lord. When the listener verbalizes what he has heard and then immediately hears the person guiding the process say, "That was really powerful," or "The Lord has taken this matter several levels deeper," or even simply, "That sounds like the Lord's voice to me," the listener gains courage and is inspired to continue. Often, sharing a passage of Scripture that corresponds to what he has heard encourages the listener.

Am I good enough to get something from Jesus?

Sometimes an answer from Jesus raises another question. Responding to what Jesus has just said—especially when we don't like it, don't agree with it, or it just doesn't make sense—frequently results in a much longer stream of revelation. After passing through a period where I was struggling with my task of writing, I had this conversation with the Lord:

Me: I am grateful that writing began to flow yesterday. I should try Clinton's method of outlining first and then writing together with you.

Jesus: I want to help you with this book.

The Lord was trying to tell me something deep here, but not grasping the significance, I went on to my next question. The Lord, however, came back to the same idea.

Me: Clinton keeps asking me why I am doing this and what I am learning.

Jesus: I want to do a project together with you.

6. Lehman, *Immanuel Approach*, 183.

Me:	Wow. That is quite amazing.
Jesus:	Why do you find that amazing?
Me:	Because I am not important enough for you to want to do something with me. Hmm. I can see this comment reveals my sense of unworthiness. I think I have to be good enough to get something from you. What if it only has to do with your desire, not with how good I am?
Jesus:	Your thoughts about things being dependent on how good you are, are a shackle that you need to throw away. This kind of thinking is greatly limiting.

The cycle of listening and verbalizing answers should continue until the listener has had enough. When the process is over, I normally check in with the listener to find out how he is doing emotionally. After listening to God about a painful family situation, Sayed said, "I feel peace that cannot be expressed in words." Sometimes the emotions, such as tears, are obvious. Sometimes the person says, "I don't know why I am crying. I don't feel bad." Other times, the person needs a moment to figure out how he is feeling emotionally.

It is helpful to remind the listener to hold on to the answers that he has received. I often hand him some paper and a pen and encourage him to write down what just happened.

Test It Later

Listening is not the stage for analysis. Testing whether what we received came from God or not comes after the listening process is over. Trying to test the veracity of what I have heard while listening is like trying to understand the digestive process while eating my mother's lemon meringue pie. Somehow, it spoils the moment. The testing process is important, but it usually cannot be done during the listening process.

One test is the emotional response. Hearing from God frequently produces a change in emotional state. Sensations of peace or lightness are very common reactions. Another test is the quality of the content. I call this the freshness test—when God speaks, what he has to say is usually new and fresh. Many times, God addresses an issue much deeper than the listener's initial question. We will discuss testing more in chapter 5.

A dull encounter

Rarely do I sit down with a person and the person does not have a genuine encounter with the Lord, but Masud was one such person. Since this was his first listening experience, I asked him to think up a question to ask God beforehand. His question was: "How do I please God?" That seemed to be a bit too generic for me, but I decided to go with it anyway. I led him in a reflective prayer in which he saw himself in a beautiful place and then found Jesus there. He told me that he saw Jesus come in the form of his father. I didn't know what to make of this since I could not immediately think of a biblical parallel. Other warning signs were that he didn't find the listening experience to be either happy or sad and he didn't receive an answer to his question.

Since there was no answer to his question nor a change in his emotions, I suspected he was not hearing the Lord. Under my breath, I prayed a prayer binding the powers of darkness, and then, after a little bit of conversation, I suggested we try again. This time, he burst out with "I need to repent." He prayed a heartfelt prayer of repentance for the corrupt behavior that his employer had been obliging him to engage in. I am not entirely sure how God spoke to Masud in this situation. Did Masud realize he couldn't fake an experience with God, and so he decided to confess the sin he knew was hindering his relationship with God? Did God speak to him by convicting him right then about his actions? Had God already been speaking to him, and this listening experience provided the safety he needed to talk about his struggle? I don't know the answers, but this experience called him to grow and face the issue that was between him and the Lord. True listening leads to growth.

Will God Ever Not Answer Us?

God is not a supernatural information source, providing information to us at the snap of our fingers. God will not allow himself to be used for our own selfish ends. I may ask God how to invest my money in the stock market. Depending on where my heart is, he may give me wise investment advice, or he may address deeper issues of greed or fear of lack. God speaks but is not obliged to give us the information we want to hear.

Sometimes we have blockages we must work through before we can listen to God with ease. The Lord may be more interested in helping us work through those blockages than in giving us the specific answers we seek. It may seem that the Lord is silent, but perhaps he is simply waiting for us to ask if anything in our hearts prevents us from hearing what he wants to say.

Sometimes the issue troubling us is beyond our comprehension. As a child, I listened in on adult conversations and heard concepts I didn't understand. When I heard about someone who had a baby out of wedlock, I pressed for explanation. Unfortunately for me, I was told, "You'll understand when you are older." Though that answer was deeply annoying for an inherently curious child, it was appropriate for my level of understanding. Similarly, our heavenly Father may not always give us the information we seek, but he will always respond to us lovingly and graciously.

Sometimes the questions in our hearts turn out simply to be a vehicle to bring us into communion with Jesus. Our questions drive us to God, but as we converse with him, he reveals the matters that are on his heart. By the end of the conversation, we may discover our own questions are no longer relevant. We can listen to God at any time on any subject, but God may not answer our questions in the way we expect.[7]

And sometimes we will make mistakes. We'll address the matter of mistakes in chapter 5.

When God speaks, is it always words? What about pictures? The next two chapters explore receiving communication from God in the form of pictures.

---

7. Job asked God many questions. God did respond to him, but God never answered the questions Job put to him. When he finally heard God's answer, Job repented "in dust and ashes" (Job 42:6) for speaking about things he did not understand. It is not wrong to ask God questions, but we must be prepared for the answers God wants to give.

Chapter 3

Does God Speak Through Dreams?

Dreams in the Bible

WE CAN'T TALK ABOUT listening to God without discussing the topic of dreams. People through the ages have looked to dreams for guidance.[1] Does God speak in dreams? If he does, why are they so difficult to understand? Are there any guidelines we can follow for interpreting our dreams?

The Bible mentions dreams over ninety times and records more than twenty full-length dreams. The majority of references to dreams are given in the context of receiving direction from God. In fact, God unequivocally declares that he speaks to people in dreams. "Then the LORD came down in a pillar of cloud; he stood at the entrance to the tent and summoned Aaron and Miriam. When the two of them stepped forward, he said, 'Listen to my words: When there is a prophet among you, I, the LORD, reveal myself to them in visions, I speak to them in dreams'" (Num 12:5–6).

Through dreams, God speaks and reveals hidden things. Strangely, he often reveals these things in the form of a riddle—something that takes some ingenuity to figure out. If we read on in this passage, we see that Moses was a special case. "But this is not true of my servant Moses; he is faithful in all my house. With him I speak face to face, clearly and not in

---

1. The book of Job is thought to be the oldest book in the Bible. In this book, dreams are mentioned several times, most notably Job 33:14–15. King Saul also sought guidance from dreams (1 Sam 28:6), and when God stopped communicating with him in this manner, he was distressed (v.15).

riddles; he sees the form of the LORD. Why then were you not afraid to speak against my servant Moses?" (Num 12:7–8).

Moses enjoyed clear, unhindered communication with God. Most people, however, often experience an element of riddle in God's communication, and this element shows up most clearly when we engage with our dreams.

As a child, I asked why we read about God speaking to people through dreams in the Bible, but we don't hear people talking about this today. I was told that now we have the Holy Spirit, and so we don't need to rely on dreams for direction. The Bible, however, teaches the opposite. "In the last days, God says, I will pour out my Spirit on all people. Your sons and daughters will prophesy, your young men will see visions, your old men will dream dreams. Even on my servants, both men and women, I will pour out my Spirit in those days, and they will prophesy" (Acts 2:17–18).[2]

The pouring out of the Holy Spirit at Pentecost results in more God-given dreams, not fewer. If we want to learn about listening to God, we cannot avoid talking about dreams. Let's look at one God-given dream.

Catastrophic Crash

After our team's bimonthly Bible study, Patrick and I fell into conversation about hearing God's voice. This led to a lunch invite several days later to continue the conversation. There, Patrick told me how he had been asking God to speak to him, and he expected God would speak to him through a dream. He then had a troubling dream, a dream that was repeated on two separate nights. I wrote down the dream as Patrick told it to me:

> Patrick saw his respected colleagues sitting in the front of a mini-van. Joseph, a ministry leader, was driving the van way too fast, and the vehicle crashed into a brick wall head-on. Those in the front seats were totally obliterated. Patrick himself was in the back of the vehicle and climbed out uninjured. He tried to call emergency services on his phone but couldn't get through.

Patrick was quite disturbed by this dream, thinking God might be showing him that his colleagues were going to be killed in an accident.

---

2. This is a quote from Joel 2:28–29. Note the Hebrew parallelisms in this passage: sons and daughters, young men and old men, men and women. God is saying that all people will receive revelation in the form of prophecy, visions, and dreams. God is not saying that dreams are only for old men.

Since Patrick had been asking God to speak to him through a dream, and since he had the same dream on two nights, I was certain that this dream was from the Lord. But I had no clue as to what the dream might mean. The only thing I could tell Patrick was that most dreams are symbolic and therefore need to be interpreted. Due to the symbolic nature of dreams, the dream was probably not saying that Patrick's colleagues would be killed.

That evening, as I was journaling about this conversation, suddenly the pieces all fit together.

> The minivan represented the ministry Patrick was involved in. This ministry was headed to a figurative brick wall due to Joseph's reckless driving. Patrick was not the driver; in fact, he was way in the back of the vehicle. So this impending crash would not be Patrick's fault. The fact that Patrick could not phone emergency services meant that he would not be able to help in this situation.

At the time, I was not clear what the obliteration of Patrick's colleagues meant. I assumed they were symbols for another one of Patrick's ministry involvements. Now, with the advantage of hindsight, I believe that the dream was telling Patrick that those in the front seat of the vehicle would be removed from the ministry scene. I emailed Patrick with my reflections, but I wasn't entirely sure how Patrick should take this dream. One possibility was that the dream was a warning from God, sent to prepare Patrick mentally and emotionally for upcoming events in this ministry.

More than two years later, I touched base with Patrick again when I asked for permission to include his story in this book. By this time, Joseph and the other colleagues who were sitting in the front seat had left the country. The ministry itself ran into a severe obstacle, necessitating the vacating of its premises and a move to another location. I believe this dream was given by God in response to Patrick's prayer that God would speak to him. It was a predictive dream that, in figurative terms, foretold events that took place more than two years later.

What Are Dreams?

The Bible warns us against uncritically accepting others' reports of dreams as messages from God.

> How long will this continue in the hearts of these lying prophets, who prophesy the delusions of their own minds? They think the

dreams they tell one another will make my people forget my name, just as their ancestors forgot my name through Baal worship. Let the prophet who has a dream recount the dream, but let the one who has my word speak it faithfully. For what has straw to do with grain?" declares the LORD. (Jer 23:26–28)[3]

If some dreams—but not all—contain messages directly from God, then what exactly are dreams? When a person dreams, the body is inactivated by the sleep state, and so the soul gives its full attention to the activity of the human spirit. I believe then that dreams are the soul observing and processing events from the perspective of the human spirit and the spiritual realm. (See chapter 6 for a further explanation of the body, soul, and human spirit and how the human spirit interacts with the spiritual realm.) There may be a lot of insight in dreams, even in dreams that do not contain explicit messages from God, because the soul is looking at life events through the eyes of the human spirit and is not distracted by what is going on in the body. Since the soul is paying attention to what is going on in the spiritual realm through the eyes of the human spirit, the soul frequently tunes in to what God is saying while one is dreaming (Job 33:14–15).

Why Riddles?

Why are dreams so hard to understand? Wouldn't it be better if God just spoke to us plainly and not in riddles? Jesus's disciples asked a similar question about his teaching. "The disciples came to him and asked, 'Why do you speak to the people in parables?'" (Matt 13:10).

The answer can be found in the previous verse, "Whoever has ears, let them hear." Jesus knew that not everyone had a heart to listen to his words. Some people were opposed to what he had to say. Some were simply not ready to take in his teaching. Still others were eager to learn. They came to him with questions and pressed in deeper for understanding. Jesus responded to the latter group by giving them more clarity.

---

3. It is unclear what exactly is happening in this passage. I see at least three possibilities: (a) some dreams are given by lying spirits seeking to draw these people away from God; (b) all dreams are accurate, though symbolic, representations of truth, but here the prophets were interpreting them incorrectly; or (c) the prophets were simply making up prophecies and claiming they had dreams to support what they were saying. I lean toward thinking that all dreams contain truth if the dream is interpreted correctly. Regardless of which option is correct, as in all means of listening to God, we must check that what we receive matches with the teaching of Scripture.

Dreams perform the same sifting process. God may have something to say that you really don't want to hear. He may have a subject to discuss that you have not thought about before. He may desire you to look at things from another viewpoint. Dreams provide a means to demonstrate that you have ears to hear what he has to say.

A Quick Course in Dream Interpretation

Dream interpretation is a complicated matter, and many books have been written on the subject. In this section, I list six questions you can ask to help interpret your dreams and hear what God is saying to you through them. Start by writing out your dream and giving it a title. The title you choose is not that important; the title is simply a mental handle to help you grasp the content of the dream. Since "interpretations belong to God," applying your intellect alone will not guarantee you will find the correct interpretation.[4] You need to seek God's help.

We will apply our six questions to the three dreams from the Bible given below and to the Catastrophic Crash dream given above.

> **Squeezing Grapes:** So the chief cupbearer told Joseph his dream. He said to him, "In my dream I saw a vine in front of me, and on the vine were three branches. As soon as it budded, it blossomed, and its clusters ripened into grapes. Pharaoh's cup was in my hand, and I took the grapes, squeezed them into Pharaoh's cup and put the cup in his hand." "This is what it means," Joseph said to him. "The three branches are three days. Within three days Pharaoh will lift up your head and restore you to your position, and you will put Pharaoh's cup in his hand, just as you used to do when you were his cupbearer. (Gen 40:9–13)

> **Skinny Cows:** When two full years had passed, Pharaoh had a dream: He was standing by the Nile, when out of the river there came up seven cows, sleek and fat, and they grazed among the reeds. After them, seven other cows, ugly and gaunt, came up out of the Nile and stood beside those on the riverbank. And the cows

---

4. Joseph articulated this thought to the cupbearer and baker (Gen 40:8). To Pharaoh, he said, "I cannot [interpret the dream] but God will give Pharaoh the answer he desires" (Gen 41:16). Daniel's answer to King Nebuchadnezzar was similarly humble. "No wise man, enchanter, magician or diviner can explain to the king the mystery he has asked about, but there is a God in heaven who reveals mysteries. He has shown King Nebuchadnezzar what will happen in days to come" (Dan 2:27–28).

that were ugly and gaunt ate up the seven sleek, fat cows. Then Pharaoh woke up. He fell asleep again and had a second dream: Seven heads of grain, healthy and good, were growing on a single stalk. After them, seven other heads of grain sprouted—thin and scorched by the east wind. The thin heads of grain swallowed up the seven healthy, full heads. Then Pharaoh woke up; it had been a dream. (Gen 41:1–7)

The Barley Loaf: Gideon arrived just as a man was telling a friend his dream. "I had a dream," he was saying. "A round loaf of barley bread came tumbling into the Midianite camp. It struck the tent with such force that the tent overturned and collapsed." His friend responded, "This can be nothing other than the sword of Gideon son of Joash, the Israelite. God has given the Midianites and the whole camp into his hands." (Judg 7:13–14)

Question 1: Is the dream symbolic or literal?

Most dreams are symbolic. They deal with things like skinny cows eating fat cows and a little loaf of bread overturning an army tent. Such symbols must be interpreted correctly for the dream to make any sense. In literal dreams, events happen just as they would in real life, and no interpretation is necessary. If even one element of a lifelike dream is symbolic, then the whole dream must be interpreted as symbolic. We know that the Squeezing Grapes dream is symbolic because the many steps from grapes to wine have all been compressed into one. The Catastrophic Crash dream is symbolic because, while car crashes are common, a vehicle crashing head on into a brick wall is extremely unlikely. Furthermore, it would be highly unlikely that the specific passengers in Patrick's dream would all be riding in a vehicle together.

The robeless judge, a literal dream

Literal dreams are rare, and I remember only one that I have had in my life. At the time, I worked at a factory outside Toronto, and when I couldn't carpool, I took a commuter train to my place of work. Due to a miscommunication between the ticket agent and myself, one day, I ended up traveling past my legal stop. On that day, the ticket checker happened to check my ticket. Despite my protestations, I was fined eighty dollars for traveling illegally. I didn't think that was fair, but my only option for redress was to go to court. I decided to pursue that option.

Before the court appearance, I had a dream. In the dream, I was in court. The judge, a small-framed man with pallid skin, dismissed the case against me. I noted that the judge was not wearing a black robe, something I assumed all judges wore. Although I didn't understand it at the time, this was a literal dream showing me what would soon happen. When the day of the court appearance came, the judge, a small-framed man with pallid skin, asked a couple of questions and then dismissed the case against me. Instead of the expected robe, the judge was wearing a suit and tie.

Solomon's literal dream

Solomon also had a literal dream.

> At Gibeon the Lord appeared to Solomon during the night in a dream, and God said, "Ask for whatever you want me to give you." Solomon answered, "So give your servant a discerning heart to govern your people and to distinguish between right and wrong." The Lord was pleased that Solomon had asked for this. So God said to him, "I will do what you have asked. I will give you a wise and discerning heart, so that there will never have been anyone like you, nor will there ever be." Then Solomon awoke—and he realized it had been a dream. (Excerpts from 1 Kgs 3:5–15.)

Literal dreams like these do not require interpretation. Much thought, however, is required to understand symbolic dreams. The remaining questions, except for Question 6, apply to symbolic dreams.

Question 2: Is the dreamer a participant or an observer?

In the Squeezing Grapes dream, the cupbearer is a participant, the main character. Without him, the dream would not make sense. On the other hand, in the Skinny Cows dream, Pharaoh doesn't even play a minor role. He is simply an observer. When the dreamer is the main character, the dream has a message for the life of the person who dreamed. In the rare case when the dreamer is purely an observer, we can ask if the dream contains a message for someone else. Pharaoh's Skinny Cows dream contains a message of impending famine for the entire region. (The interpretation is given in Gen 41:25–32.)

In most dreams (more than 95 percent), the dreamer is a participant, indicating that the dream is about the life of the dreamer.[5] Sometimes the dreamer is both a participant and an observer. In the Catastrophic Crash dream, Patrick's role was minimal. All he did was try to call emergency services, and even that failed. This was a dream about future events, but since Patrick had a role to play in the dream, I believe the dream was primarily intended for Patrick.

Question 3: What is the main action?

In the Squeezing Grapes dream, the main action is serving wine to Pharaoh. In the Skinny Cows dream, the main action is something good being consumed by something bad. In the Barley Loaf dream, the main action is destruction of something large by something small and innocuous. In the Catastrophic Crash, the main action is a sudden and disastrous halt. The main action in dreams is a symbolic representation of an action in real life.

Question 4: What is the main emotion?

Unfortunately, the Bible rarely attaches emotions to the dreams it records. We cannot, therefore, use the biblical dreams listed above to determine the role of emotion. The emotion in the dream normally represents the same emotion in real life. If you have a dream and cannot connect to how the dream might relate to your life, look for a place in real life where you have the same emotion as the emotion in the dream.

Three Pauls

In real life, I was at a conference for our team. At that time, I knew three people named Paul. I'll call them Paul X, Paul Y, and Paul Z. Paul X was a retired former team member and not present at the conference. Paul Y was a senior team member and someone I appreciated. Paul Z was a guest at the conference. I dreamed that I was irritated at Paul X. On waking, I could not figure this out; I had nothing against Paul X, and he was not even present at the conference. However, when I matched the emotion in the dream to my emotion in real life, I realized I was irritated at Paul Z. If I had ears to hear,

---

5. Virkler, *Christian Dream Interpretation*, 4.

the dream was showing me through a riddle that I needed to process my negative emotions toward Paul Z.

Hitting as hard as she could

Shazneen dreamed she was holding a child. Another person came and took the child away from her and was beating it. Shazneen protested, to no avail. The other person then hurled the child back at Shazneen. Shazneen responded by hitting the other person as hard as she could. She wanted to hit the person even harder but could not. This dream was part of a series of three dreams that shared the theme of fighting against someone but being unable to injure her opponent.

We discussed this dream, but neither of us could figure out the meaning until I asked about the primary emotion. Shazneen told me that the primary emotions were anger and grief. I then probed, "Where do you experience the same emotions in real life?" Shazneen grew silent. She had discovered the meaning and was not ready to share further that day. Later, she revealed the pain that a family member had been causing her. I believe these dreams were God's invitation to process the anger and grief in her heart.

Question 5: What do the main symbols mean?

This is the hardest part of dream interpretation and where you need the Lord's help. In the Squeezing Grapes dream, the main symbols are a vine with three branches, a cup, and Pharaoh. Joseph tells us that the three branches indicate three days. The cup represents the cupbearer's profession. Pharaoh represents himself. In the Skinny Cows dream, the seven fat cows represent seven good years, and the seven skinny cows represent seven bad years. In the Barley Loaf dream, the tent represents the Midianite army, and the loaf represents the small band of Gideon's men. In the Catastrophic Crash dream, the vehicle represents a ministry, and the people inside represent themselves.

Other considerations

As seen in the biblical examples above, numbers in dreams almost always refer to the same number in real life. But it takes wisdom and revelation from God to know what that number refers to. Do the three branches refer to three days or three months? Do the seven cows refer to seven years or seven kingdoms? Repeated dreams are especially significant. Patrick had the Catastrophic Crash dream twice. Pharaoh had two very similar dreams, and Joseph explained, "The reason the dream was given to Pharaoh in two forms is that the matter has been firmly decided by God, and God will do it soon" (Gen 41:32). In addition to numbers and repeated dreams, angels (Matt 1:20–21) and voices (Dan 4:13–16) in dreams should be given careful attention.

Question 6: What is the purpose of this dream?

This is the most important question we should ask when interpreting our dreams. Why did God give me this dream? What was his purpose? This is the question we will address in the next section.

God's Purposes in Dreams

As we look at how God spoke to people in the Bible, we can find several purposes of dreams.

Revealing the future

Dreams may reveal future events so that we prepare for them effectively. The Squeezing Grapes dream revealed what would happen to the cupbearer in three days' time. The Skinny Cows dream showed that first prosperity and then famine would come to the region, enabling the people to adequately prepare.

Warning

Dreams show us where we need to take corrective action. God warned Abimelech that he needed to return Abraham's wife (Gen 20:3–8). When Jacob fled deceitfully from his uncle Laban, Laban was warned in a dream about his plan to harm Jacob (Gen 31:19–29). The magi were warned against going back to Herod in a dream (Matt 2:12).

Direction

God gives direction to people in dreams. In the New Testament, Joseph was told to take Mary as his wife in a dream (Matt 1:20–21). Joseph was also guided to flee to Egypt (Matt 2:13), guided when to return (Matt 2:19–20), and guided where to return to (Matt 2:22), all in dreams. Pilate was given direction through his wife's dream that Jesus was innocent and Pilate should have nothing to do with him (Matt 27:19), direction that Pilate did not heed.

We must be careful, however, when assuming all dreams give direction. Sometimes dreams only highlight the problem, and then we must pray and seek wisdom about what to do. Pharaoh's Skinny Cows dream did not tell Pharaoh what to do; it only revealed the coming calamity. But Joseph grasped the situation and advised Pharaoh how to save his kingdom from famine. Similarly, Nebuchadnezzar's dream of a great tree that was later cut down did not tell Nebuchadnezzar what to do (Dan 4:4–27). Instead, Daniel bravely urged the king to repent.

Revealing our deepest thoughts

Many times, we find it difficult to admit to ourselves our deepest thoughts, fears, and emotions. Dreams are a mirror, revealing these thoughts to us if we are willing to look.

> I looked, and there before me stood a tree in the middle of the land. Its height was enormous. The tree grew large and strong and its top touched the sky; it was visible to the ends of the earth. Its leaves were beautiful, its fruit abundant, and on it was food for all. Under it the wild animals found shelter, and the birds lived in its branches; from it every creature was fed. (Dan 4:10b–12)

Nebuchadnezzar's dream revealed his perceptions about his own greatness and, if he had ears to hear, the depths of his pride. Nebuchadnezzar was not willing to hear and faced serious consequences.

Twelve months later, as the king was walking on the roof of the royal palace of Babylon, he said, "Is not this the great Babylon I have built as the royal residence, by my mighty power and for the glory of my majesty?" Even as the words were on his lips, a voice came from heaven, "This is what is decreed for you, King Nebuchadnezzar: Your royal authority has been taken from you. You will be driven away from people and will live with the wild animals; you will eat grass like the ox. Seven times will pass by for you until you acknowledge that the Most High is sovereign over all kingdoms on earth and gives them to anyone he wishes." (Dan 4:29–32)

Bringing us into wholeness

What did God desire from Nebuchadnezzar? Having an amazing dream and receiving an interesting interpretation does not do much good if it does not produce change. God's desire for us in all his communication is to bring us into wholeness, and dreams are one of the means that God uses to achieve this end. But we can only move into wholeness if we are willing to make some changes. As we seek to determine God's purpose in a dream, we can ask ourselves, "What is the call to action in this dream?" If we can find no specific call to action, we can still ask the Lord, "What can I take from this dream and integrate into my life?"

Three Steps to Nothingness—A Call to Action

Fazil, mentioned in the first chapter, has a deep heart for the Lord and has had numerous significant dreams. Several years ago, he had a dream that accurately foreshadowed the loss of his job and that of several of his colleagues. But this time, he had a dream that he could not make sense of. He called me and told me the dream, hoping for an interpretation. I immediately got out a pen and paper and began recording the dream as he told it to me. Even after writing down this dream, however, the meaning was totally unintelligible.

In Fazil's dream, he saw himself walking along a path. Some people behind him on the path overtook him and went on ahead of him. He passed others as he walked along. Then he came to a set of three steps. The steps seemed to go into nothingness.

Fazil must have sensed the significance of this dream, so he requested that I ask God for the interpretation. I promised to pray but did not have a lot of faith. The next morning, during my prayer time, I was reflecting on this dream when, suddenly, the meaning became clear. Walking on the path represented Fazil's journey through life. Some of those behind Fazil in age went on ahead of him and passed away. He, on the other hand, overtook others as he walked toward eternity. The space above the steps represented what happens after death—something that cannot be seen. The three steps represented a time period, most likely three years.

As soon as I grasped the meaning, I was horrified at the idea of sharing it with Fazil. In a culture where doctors and family members do not even tell a patient that the situation is terminal, how could I tell my friend that God was telling him he would die in three years? Since I did not know what to do and was at such an advanced level of spiritual maturity (well, maybe not), I attempted to put the matter out of my mind by turning to my Bible reading for that morning. I had been reading through the book of Genesis and had just reached the point where Joseph interpreted the dreams of Pharaoh's cupbearer and baker (Gen 40). God was telling me that I could not keep silent and would have to tell Fazil the meaning of his dream, even though the meaning was not pleasant.

That day, I called him and very tentatively shared with him the meaning as I understood it. I also shared that sometimes a dream is not a statement of what will happen, but a warning of what might happen if a person continues on the path he is on. Fazil was suffering from numerous health issues at the time, many of which stemmed from being significantly overweight. I wondered if God was telling him he needed to make lifestyle changes if he wanted to live longer than three years.[6]

The rest of the story

In the years following, I frequently wondered if Fazil would suddenly drop dead from a heart attack. More than five years later, I finally got the courage to bring up the matter. Fazil then told me the back story. Despite being a strong believer and one through whom God had worked in some amazing

6. Since that time, I have come to realize that for God to warn someone in the prime of life that he will die soon is an extremely rare event. If anyone thinks God has given them such a warning, I would urge much caution, humility, and lots of checking with wise spiritual mentors.

ways, Fazil had a secret addiction to cigarettes. He needed to keep it secret because use of tobacco was a punishable offense in our organization. I told him the dream's interpretation, and later that same day, he attended a Pentecostal-style meeting. He really doubted all he was seeing was real, but despite his doubts, he came under the power of the Holy Spirit. Later in the meeting, the speaker offered a special prayer for those who needed deliverance from addictions. Fazil was too ashamed, due to his previous doubts, to go forward. Yet God touched him even though he stayed in his seat, and he was instantly delivered from his addiction. I am happy to say that Fazil is still alive and has even lost some weight. Fazil's dream was a call to action.

Video on Demand?

After trying to understand my dreams and the dreams of others for almost twenty years, I am convinced that God does speak through dreams and speak very powerfully. The main problem with dreams is we must be asleep to hear God's voice through them. That is a little inconvenient when one needs God's immediate insight. The other problem with dreams is we do not usually have much control over what we dream about.[7] Dreams are not well suited to receiving answers to specific questions. What if we could see things God shows us in response to our questions while we are awake? In the next chapter, we explore the concept of visions.

7. The topic of dream incubation is beyond the scope of this chapter. See https://en.wikipedia.org/wiki/Dream_incubation for more information.

Chapter 4

Seeing Visions

Rocks and Cactus

FAYEZ WAS PRAYING FOR a woman whose husband has been living abroad for ten years. Over the last two years, the husband had not sent any money to support the family. The woman was experiencing financial difficulty and so asked Fayez to pray that her husband would return and take care of the family. Fayez saw a vision of a barren, rocky place with lots of cactus. He couldn't bring himself to pray that her husband would return. Fayez believed God was showing him that her husband had married another woman and would never come back.

Visions Are Very Common

God commonly speaks through visions. In addition to well-known prophets like Isaiah, Ezekiel, and Daniel, Abraham (Gen 15:1–21), Jacob (Gen 46:2–4), and Samuel (1 Sam 3:1–15) all saw visions. The New Testament records that Zechariah (Luke 1:22), Ananias (Acts 9:10), Cornelius (Acts 10:3), Peter (Acts 10:17), and Paul (Acts 16:9; 18:9) saw visions as well.

The absence of visions usually corresponds to a time of apostasy. When Samuel was a child, the Bible states, "In those days the word of the LORD was rare; there were not many visions" (1 Sam 3:1). This is not surprising when we look at the time in which Samuel was living. The religious leaders of the time used their positions of authority for their personal benefit, completely disregarding the commands of the Lord. They were also immoral, demonstrating an attitude of deep rebellion (1 Sam 2:12–16, 22).

The book of Acts records several visions, and from this, we can infer that visions were very common to New Testament followers of Jesus. When an angel physically appeared to Peter and released him from prison, Peter assumed it was just another vision, probably a vision showing him symbolically what would happen in the future. It took him several minutes to figure out that no, this time, he wasn't seeing a vision, and he was out of jail (Acts 12:6–11).

Paul frequently saw visions, and he relied on these for direction.[1] "One night the Lord spoke to Paul in a vision: 'Do not be afraid; keep on speaking, do not be silent. For I am with you, and no one is going to attack and harm you, because I have many people in this city.' So Paul stayed in Corinth for a year and a half, teaching them the word of God" (Acts 18:9–11).

I believe many modern-day Christians have had visions too but have not interpreted them as such, perhaps out of the mistaken belief that they are not worthy to receive something so dramatic as a vision.

Example: Fighting wild creatures

After saying good night to my wife, I often sit in a chair in the living room and pray for a while. My thoughts frequently go to a bustee[2] near our home, a place where some colleagues and I started a prayer ministry. One night, I saw myself standing in the center of the bustee, holding a large bowl containing the love of God. As I poured out from this bowl, a giant snake reared up to attack me. Then several lions came to oppose me. The lions were followed by an indistinct black creature. I fought all these creatures with a shining sword in each hand. After the excitement of the battle, it took me a few moments to calm down enough to get back to pouring out the love of God from the bowl. Then I caught a glimpse of what it means to be in Christ, and I began to increase in size, enabling me to pour out the love of God on a larger area.

---

1. Paul's visions are listed here: vision that led to his conversion (Acts 9:3–8); Macedonian vision (Acts 16:6–10); vision at Corinth (Acts 18:9–11); angelic appearance that could have been a vision (Acts 27:23–24); caught up to paradise—assuming Paul is referring to himself in this passage (2 Cor 12:1–4).

2. "Bustee" is a South Asian term for a settlement or slum.

What Is a Vision?

A vision is something seen or perceived.[3] Although many modern writers draw a distinction between "dreams" and "visions," the Bible frequently uses these two words interchangeably. Examples include Num 12:6; Job 7:14; 33:15; and Dan 2:28, 45. It is helpful for me to understand "vision" as a broader word that refers to many different types of seeing, including dreams. As with dreams, visions are a normal part of God's communication with people, according to Num 12:6 and Acts 2:17. Also, as with dreams, visions frequently need interpretation.

Common Misconceptions about Visions

For much of my life, I assumed that receiving a vision was an extremely rare occurrence, and that it was a tremendous, life-changing event for those who experienced one. I assumed that visions were accompanied by overpowering emotion, primarily fear. I assumed that visions could not be doubted. I assumed they were always totally clear and needed no interpretation. We'll examine these false assumptions below.

Misconception 1: Visions come with overpowering emotion

Daniel's vision (Dan 10:8) left him deathly pale and helpless. However, not all visions result in powerful emotions, and most visions may easily be dismissed. In the book of Acts, God told Ananias in a vision to go and pray for Saul, the great persecutor.

> In Damascus there was a disciple named Ananias. The Lord called to him in a vision, "Ananias!" "Yes, Lord," he answered. The Lord told him, "Go to the house of Judas on Straight Street and ask for a man from Tarsus named Saul, for he is praying. In a vision he has seen a man named Ananias come and place his hands on him to restore his sight." "Lord," Ananias answered, "I have heard many reports about this man and all the harm he has done to your holy people in Jerusalem. And he has come here with authority from the chief priests to arrest all who call on your name." But the Lord said to Ananias, "Go! This man is my chosen instrument to proclaim my name to the Gentiles and their kings and to the people

3. Arnold, "Vision(s)."

of Israel. I will show him how much he must suffer for my name."
(Acts 9:10–16)

There is no record that Ananias was frightened by the vision itself, though he was certainly uncomfortable with the task given him.

When Peter saw a vision of a sheet being let down from heaven (Acts 10:11–16) there is no record of fear over the fact that he saw a vision. More likely, the primary emotion would have been revulsion over what he saw. Similarly, there is no record of strong emotion in Jeremiah's visions of the almond branch and boiling pot (Jer 1:11–15) or in Amos's visions of a man with a plumb line (Amos 7:7–9) or basket of ripe fruit (Amos 8:1–2). We will look at some of these visions more fully below.

Misconception 2: Visions cannot be doubted

If Ananias were convinced that God was speaking to him, we would not expect him to respond with an expression of doubt regarding God's direction: "Lord, I have heard many reports about this man and all the harm he has done to your holy people in Jerusalem. And he has come here with authority from the chief priests to arrest all who call on your name." Like other forms of God's voice, visions can easily be doubted.

In this vision, we learn what to do with our doubts: ask questions and carry on the conversation. As Ananias continued to talk with the Lord, not only did his doubts evaporate, but he understood in a deeper way God's plans for Saul.

Although there is no record that God's voice to Samuel came in the form of a vision (1 Sam 16:2), we see Samuel employing the same tactic when he doubted. He asked a question and carried on the conversation. As the conversation proceeded, Samuel received the courage to carry out God's instructions.

Misconception 3: Visions always come with great clarity

For most of my life, I assumed that visions came with great clarity. When I began to lead others to hear God's voice, I discovered that God's voice often comes in the form of a vision, and this vision is not completely clear much of the time. When I asked God to open my eyes so that I could see into the spiritual realm, I experienced the same thing. I would see something, but I wasn't sure if what I was seeing was really a vision from God.

Example: A tightly bound figure

Jim came into my office to talk about project-related matters. As he sat down in front of me, I briefly saw a faint vision of a tightly bound person. At the end of our work-related conversation, with much trepidation, I shared what I had seen and asked Jim if it meant anything to him. It did. Jim was feeling constrained about sharing his faith due to the potential risks it would bring to the organization he was working for. Sharing this vision brought us into a deeper prayer time than otherwise would have occurred.

Example: A bleeding heart

As I was chatting with Laura, I saw a picture of a bleeding heart. I wasn't sure if this was just me or from the Lord. A couple of days later, when we had more time to talk, I mentioned what I had seen to her. Immediately, tears came to her eyes. Over the next couple of hours, she shared a long-standing pain she had been carrying.

Especially as we are starting out learning to see visions, our visions are often not very clear. Most of the time, we are not sure if what we are seeing is a vision from God or a figment of our own imagination. It is important, however, to pay attention to what we are seeing, describe it in words to God (or perhaps to the person we are with), and then ask if it means anything.

Misconception 4: Visions are easy to understand

I used to assume that if I ever received a vision, the meaning would be readily apparent. Visions, however, are often figurative. We may be tempted to dismiss the visions we receive as figments of our imaginations simply because we cannot make sense of them.

One day, Peter fell into a trance (Acts 10:10) and saw a vision of non-kosher animals coming down from heaven on a sheet. He heard a voice telling him to kill them and eat them. I can imagine Peter dismissing this vision, saying to himself, *Wow, I was praying and then, silly me, I fell asleep. I really ought to be more disciplined in prayer. While asleep, I had a very strange dream. It could not have been from God because, in it, I was told to eat unclean animals.*

After two days, Peter understood that God had been speaking to him in symbolic terms, telling him that he could go into the houses of non-Jews, fellowship with them, and eat the non-kosher food they set before him. To Peter, eating non-kosher food would have been as repulsive as eating frogs, snakes, dogs, and monkeys would be to many people in the Western world.

Paul also had visions which required interpretation. "During the night Paul had a vision of a man of Macedonia standing and begging him, 'Come over to Macedonia and help us'" (Acts 16:9).

We, who have read the Bible many times, know the meaning of Paul's vision of the Macedonian man, and so we tend not to think about the interpretation process. When Paul had the vision, he and his companions had been facing a lack of clarity over where they should go next on their second missionary journey. They were prevented from preaching in the province of Asia and had been blocked when they tried to enter Bithynia (Acts 16:6–7). After Paul had seen the vision, his companions weighed the matter together and concluded God was directing them to go to Macedonia (Acts 16:10).[4]

Learning to Receive Visions—a Divine Coaching Session

We can prepare our hearts to receive visions once we remove the following assumptions: that visions must include powerful emotions, that they cannot be doubted, that they must come with such clarity that they cannot be dismissed, and that they need no interpretation.

Just like learning to hear God's voice in other ways, we can learn how to receive visions. In fact, we observe God coaching Jeremiah in the very same thing. In the first chapter of the book of Jeremiah, we read how God called him to be a prophet to the nations. Jeremiah protested that due to his inexperience ("I am too young"), he could not carry out this mandate. So God touched his mouth and said, "I have put my words in your mouth." Then the coaching session began. "The word of the LORD came to me: 'What do you see, Jeremiah?' 'I see the branch of an almond tree,' I replied. The LORD said to me, 'You have seen correctly, for I am watching to see that my word is fulfilled'" (Jer 1:11–12).

---

4. The Greek word translated as "concluding" in Acts 16:10 (NIV) is *sumbibazo*. In this context, the meaning is "to conclusively weigh a matter and thus direct one's actions." *Mickelson's*, s. v. "G4822 *sumbibazo*."

Jeremiah had a picture of an almond tree in his mind, and God was drawing his attention to it.[5] Since the visual cortex is in a different part of the brain than the area where words and meaning are processed, God asked Jeremiah to verbalize what he had seen.[6] Putting things into words enhances the reality of the experience and enables us to understand the importance of what we are experiencing. Then God encouraged Jeremiah by telling him that he had seen correctly; this was not just a figment of his imagination. Doubt about what we have seen can be the greatest barrier to receiving visions from God. Most of the time, the visions we receive, especially in the beginning, are like fleeting pictures. We are not quite sure what we have seen and are even less sure it is from God.

Receiving a vision from God is one thing; interpreting it is another matter. It was only as Jeremiah reflected on this picture that he heard God's word to him. The interpretation of this vision is particularly interesting. The Hebrew word for "almond tree" used here is *shâkêd*. The word for "watching" is *shôkêd*, a difference of only one vowel. In Semitic languages such as Hebrew and Arabic, the vowels are often not even written in the text. God was using a pun on the similarity between "almond" and "watching" to communicate his message to Jeremiah.[7]

In the same manner, God repeats the lesson in the next verses. This time, Jeremiah has a picture of a boiling pot, tilting away from the north. Again, God asks him what he sees. As Jeremiah explains the picture to God, God gives him the word of prophecy (Jer 1:13–14). By the time we get to Jer 24, Jeremiah knows that God has shown him the picture, and God no longer needs to tell him he has seen correctly. This time, he saw two baskets of figs in the temple. Due to the importance of verbalizing what one sees, God still asked Jeremiah to describe what he saw. As Jeremiah described the picture back to God, God gave him the meaning (Jer 24:1–10).[8]

5. While it is theoretically possible that Jeremiah was sitting outside and staring at a physical almond tree when God spoke to him, this was more likely a vision, a picture that Jeremiah saw in his mind. Why else would God tell him that he had seen correctly if it were not a vision?

6. The visual cortex processes visual information from the eyes but is also active during imagination and visualization. Vitrano, "Perception and Imagination," 2. The temporal lobe creates meanings out of sensory input and is also the area of the brain where language is processed. Javed et al., "Neuroanatomy, Cerebral Cortex."

7. Plumptre, *Jeremiah*, 11.

8. This method of receiving God's revelation is not limited to Jeremiah. God used the same procedure with Amos. In Amos 7, God shows Amos a series of pictures, each depicting disaster that will come on the people of Israel. Each time, Amos cries out to God

A Simple Process

The format of this form of revelation is simple.[9] The recipient receives a picture in his mind. God asks him to describe what he is seeing. As he describes the picture, God gives the meaning. In most cases, God's message is a symbolic interpretation of the picture.

The process for receiving visions is similar to the simple method of listening to Jesus given in chapter 2. First, we quiet our hearts; then, we fix our minds on Jesus. Then we ask him to give us a picture. After we receive the picture, we describe it back to Jesus. As we describe it back to Jesus, we ask him what it means. Sometimes, however, we still cannot understand what the picture means. In this situation, we do well to share the vision with another person and seek their input.

Praying with Beauty

I was praying with Beauty and her husband.[10] Beauty is illiterate. She asked God to give her a picture just as Jeremiah received pictures from the Lord. She saw a red rose but did not know what this could mean. I suggested that since a rose is a symbol of love, God was showing her how much he loved her. Her heart resonated with this interpretation, and her face radiated with the encouragement she felt.

Viewing the future

The next day, I was visiting with Kamal and his wife. After explaining how God spoke to Jeremiah through pictures, we quieted our hearts and asked

---

not to bring disaster, and God relents. The final picture is of a wall built true to plumb and the Lord standing beside it with a plumb line in his hand (Amos 7:7–9). Again, God asks Amos to describe what he sees. As Amos describes the picture in his mind's eye, God gives the meaning. We see the same thing in the next chapter where Amos sees a basket of ripe fruit (Amos 8:1–2).

9. Here, I am using the word "revelation" to mean something revealed by God to us personally. I am not equating what we hear in our listening experiences with the authority of Scripture. Scripture, the Bible, is revelation from God with the highest level of authority. Revelation received in our own personal listening experiences may contain error and thus does not have the same level of authority. See "Chapter 5: Mistakes and Discernment" for more on this subject.

10. English words such as Dolly, Lovely, Rosy, Sweety, Flora, and Beauty are common female names in some South Asian countries.

God to speak to us. Kamal saw what he described as an office room with a table. Others were in the room. He was standing beside the table, supervising the person behind the table. Kamal didn't understand the meaning of this vision, and I hadn't a clue either. Kamal's wife, however, understood. She explained that Kamal was seeing a vision of the church they were hoping to plant in that town. In this vision, Kamal was supervising the person who would be the leader of the new church. Both Kamal and his wife were heartened by this vision.

The Challenges of TCKs

The mentoring conversation I had with Dave centered on the unique challenges of third culture kids (TCKs). I was drawing on my own experience as an adult TCK, reflecting that learning to hear God's voice was the most helpful factor in processing my own TCK experiences. I mused to Dave that if TCKs could learn how to listen to God while they are children, that would be one of the most helpful tools they could use to process their own experiences of living in different cultures. At the end of the conversation, Dave prayed that I would find a TCK to encourage in his or her spiritual journey.

Before Dave finished his prayer, I knew just the person. Manan was a thirteen-year-old South Asian. At the age of two, he had moved with his parents to the Philippines, where his parents were studying theology. When Manan returned to his native country at age six, he was fluent in English but could hardly speak his mother tongue. The adjustment back to what was supposed to be his home country was very difficult. Now Manan was entering his teen years but still had some of the marks of that childhood experience in his life. I asked Manan if he wanted to meet with me. We began to meet, and God spoke to him through a vision.

Manan's series of visions

In one of my meetings with Manan, we looked at several passages in Scripture where God communicated through visions. Manan then closed his eyes in a posture of prayer and expectation. God spoke to him through a series of visions in his mind's eye. After each experience, he related what he saw, and we discussed the meaning together.

Vision 1

Manan saw himself at home. A cell phone was ringing, but he couldn't find it.

Manan:	All I hear is a phone ringing. But what can this mean?
Neil:	Manan, what do you think it means?
Manan:	I think it means that I have an opportunity to hear God. The opportunity is there, but I don't know how.
Neil:	Let's listen again. Re-enter that same picture where you are at home and the phone is ringing.

Vision 2

Manan reported, "The phone kept ringing and ringing. I was looking all over the house for it. I finally found it under a Bible."

Neil:	What do you think this means?
Manan:	That I should look for answers in the Bible?

We stopped to talk about it. After discussing this for a while, we re-entered the vision.

Vision 3

This time, Manan saw an app pop up on the phone. It was an ad for an institution where one could understand the Bible with the help of others.

Neil:	What does it mean?
Manan:	I should ask others for help when I read the Bible. I should share my experiences with others.

Even though it should have been totally obvious, I didn't really get the message that day as I sat with Manan. God was telling him that he needed to concentrate on reading the Bible. This is where he would find the answers to his questions at this stage in his life, and this is how he would hear God speak to him. God was also showing him that he needed to involve others in his quest for answers to his spiritual questions.

We didn't continue meeting together. Manan was a busy student, and I didn't want to pressure him to keep meeting with me. I let him know that the door was always open if he wanted to meet again. Very sadly, Manan died tragically about a year later. As I look back on this time, I see how God was tenderly reaching out to Manan and seeking to draw Manan closer to himself.

Visions and the Bible

Some are uncomfortable with the idea of God speaking to us today. Their fear stems from the idea that listening to God in the present might draw people away from the Bible. Jack Deere writes: "I wanted to preserve the unique authority of the Bible. I was afraid that if any form of divine communication other than the Bible were allowed, we would weaken the Bible's authority and eventually be led away from the Lord."[11]

My observation has been the opposite. Often, just as it was for Manan, I have observed that one of the first messages God communicates to people as they begin to learn to listen to him is precisely that they need to spend more time reading their Bible. The Bible becomes real. It is no longer a series of stories from history that seem to have little bearing on life today. The spiritual vitality they see in the Bible can be theirs as well. The net result is drawing closer to Jesus.

Visions, just like other forms of hearing God's voice, need to be tested and measured by Scripture. We'll address this subject in the next chapter.

11. Deere, *Voice of God*, 254.

Chapter 5

Mistakes and Discernment

God Told Me That I Will Get This Job

Our office was struggling, and we needed to hire an additional worker. We posted a job circular, collected applicants, and conducted a written examination. Since this was an organization with Christian goals, we asked the job seekers questions about their faith and personal devotional life. One applicant answered a question with the statement, "God told me that I will get this job." Unfortunately for her, we did not select her. While she had scored very highly, another applicant seemed to be a better all-round candidate. We hired him and have been pleased with his performance.

I know this young woman well. She loves the Lord and earnestly desires to please him. She has heard the Lord's voice correctly in other situations. Why did she get it wrong in this case? Was it a simple mistake due to the pressure of needing to find employment? Did she hear God's heart correctly, that he will provide for her, but make a mistake on the timing and the details?

Your 10:00 A.M. Appointment Won't Come

I had a busy day planned and was also scheduled to meet with one of my staff members for a coaching session. We hadn't touched base recently, and I wouldn't have been surprised if he forgot our meeting. If he forgot, I would have been grateful as that would free up sixty minutes in my schedule. That morning in my devotions, I thought I heard, "He won't come." Forty-five minutes later, he texted me to ask if our meeting was still on. Not only had he remembered, but he came. I had made a mistake in listening to God.

If we are not careful, our mistakes can have more serious consequences. Another time, as I was praying for someone with whom I met regularly, I put little pieces of information together in my mind that suggested that this man might have a secret pornography problem. Was this the Lord's insight coming to me during a time of prayer? What should I do with such information if, indeed, it did come from the Lord? It would be extremely damaging to our relationship to suggest he had such a problem if he didn't. Even if he did have a problem, he might deny it. In my next meeting with him, I decided to bring up the subject of sexual temptation in a general way and talk about how this can affect us during times of stress and pressure. By his responses, my best conclusion was that I was wrong, and pornography was not an issue he was struggling with. Although we had a solid, deep conversation and I certainly didn't accuse him of wrongdoing, afterward, I felt ashamed for making this kind of mistake in my mind.

If God truly speaks, why do mistakes sometimes occur? In the next sections, we will look at why we make mistakes, how we should respond when mistakes occur, and how we can grow in discernment.

Why We Make Mistakes

Moses was extraordinarily humble and heard God's voice with astonishing clarity. Once Miriam and Aaron, Moses's sister and brother, took offense over Moses's leadership position. "'Has the LORD spoken only through Moses?' they asked. 'Hasn't he also spoken through us?'" (Num 12:2). God's response to them tells us something about how most people experience God's voice.

> Then the LORD came down in a pillar of cloud; he stood at the entrance to the tent and summoned Aaron and Miriam. When the two of them stepped forward, he said, "Listen to my words: When there is a prophet among you, I, the LORD, reveal myself to them in visions, I speak to them in dreams. But this is not true of my servant Moses; he is faithful in all my house. With him I speak face to face, clearly and not in riddles; he sees the form of the LORD. Why then were you not afraid to speak against my servant Moses?" (Num 12:5–8)

Moses was not an ordinary prophet. Ordinary prophets see visions and dreams, both of which need to be interpreted. When God speaks to them, he usually does so in riddles—bits of information are left out so the prophet must try to understand the meaning of the riddle. As a result, the prophet does not always understand the full meaning or importance of the message he has received. With Moses, it was different. He saw God face to face. God spoke to him as he would speak to a friend (Exod 33:11).

Now it would be nice to think that since we are under the new covenant and since God has written his law on our hearts (Jer 31:33-34), we would understand God's will clearly and never make mistakes. This does not seem to be the way it works. At first, Peter could not comprehend the meaning of the vision of non-kosher animals being let down from heaven on a sheet (Acts 10:9-16). Paul and his companions struggled with direction on their second missionary journey (Acts 16:6-10). Luke and the disciples in Caesarea incorrectly advised Paul against going to Jerusalem (Acts 21:10-15).

Looking into a cloudy mirror

Paul expected that we would not see everything clearly. He looked forward to a time when there was total clarity, but that time is not the present. "For we know in part and we prophesy in part, but when completeness comes, what is in part disappears . . . For now we see only a reflection as in a mirror; then we shall see face to face. Now I know in part; then I shall know fully, even as I am fully known" (1 Cor 13:9-10, 12).

In the context of listening to God's voice, we are often hearing imperfectly, as if we were seeing something akin to a cloudy reflection in a polished bronze mirror.[1] The Bible does not give us reason to expect all our communications with God will be crystal clear.

---

1. "Mirrors were used by the ancient Egyptians as early as c. 2900 BC. These were made of polished bronze shaped into flat round discs . . . . By the time of Seneca the younger (4 BC–65), a small number of Greek mirrors were large enough to reflect a person's entire figure. Most remained quite small—less than 12 inches diameter." Lowder, "Through A Glass, Darkly."

Extending Grace to Ourselves and Others

Not surprisingly, then, we make mistakes. God does not always reveal everything in full detail. We can take a truth God reveals to us and erroneously extrapolate it to something beyond what he intended. Sometimes he only shows us the immediate next step and waits until we respond before he reveals more. At other times, we might be in too much of a hurry to get an answer to our question to really listen to the deeper things God wants to talk to us about. Sometimes our own desires cloud what God is trying to tell us.

Our lack of total clarity impels us to approach the subject of listening to God with a great deal of humility. When we make a mistake, we need to go back to Jesus and talk to him about it. We can ask, "Lord, why did I go wrong here? What was my deeper motivation? Are there desires in my heart that are making it hard to hear your voice accurately?" When we or others make a mistake in listening to God's voice, we ought to extend grace to them and ourselves. If we want to grow in hearing God's voice, we need to rise when we fall and keep walking on our journey with Jesus.

When it comes to listening to God's voice, we can face a much bigger problem than making the odd mistake here and there. We can end up listening to the wrong voice altogether.

Listening to the Wrong Voice

Sanjoy had come to faith in Jesus from a Hindu background a little over a year before we met. Prior to conversion, he had been rebellious, violent toward people in his household, and involved in drugs and gambling. His life was radically changed when Jesus came into his heart. Yet even after conversion, he still heard voices in his head. Most of these voices were silenced when a more mature Christian prayed for him one day, but Sanjoy still faced a lot of confusion when he tried to listen to the Holy Spirit.

Sanjoy found that he was constantly being told what to do and pressured to do it. This time, it wasn't a voice in his head but thoughts in his heart. When he traveled somewhere, he was told to take a bus instead of a taxi so that he would have more money to give to Jesus. As he was walking down the street, he would be told to give money to a beggar. He was told to encourage people on Facebook. He was told to go to the doctor and get checked out for a medical condition. He was told to read the Bible. He was told to go to church. He was told to fast. He was told to kneel in prayer for long periods of time.

Most of these tasks sound good or at least harmless. After all, what could be wrong with being told to read the Bible or go to church? But if one looked at the overall trajectory of these commands, something wasn't right. These commands came with a tone of harshness. They did not bring joy. At times, the tasks he was given prevented him from sleeping. He was frustrated. Sanjoy lived in fear of disobedience, thinking that if he disobeyed, he would commit the sin of blasphemy against the Holy Spirit.

Apart from several indicators that something was not quite right in Sanjoy's experience—indicators that we'll look at in the "Growing in Discernment" section below—I am cautious when anyone says he hears God's voice constantly like a stream of commands. Here's why.

A constant stream of commands

When I was in Bible college, I lived in a mobile home in a trailer park, along with many other students and their families. In the next trailer over, there was a young family with two children. One day, I saw the young son watering the garden with his father supervising. The father was giving continuous instructions like the following. "More water over there in the corner. No, do it like this. Make sure you get those plants by the side. Don't let the water run off over there. More water here. See, those plants aren't getting anything. Now put the hose here. Make sure you don't miss that spot. No, don't do it like that; do it like this."

As I looked on, I felt sorry for the boy. Why didn't the father just shut up and let his son water the garden? Why did the boy have to listen to a constant barrage of instructions? The boy needed to have the freedom to exercise his own intellect and do as he saw best, with perhaps just a short word of direction here and there. I do not believe God treats us like that father treated his son. God has given us intellect and creativity. He wants us to use and develop these capabilities. He does not want us to be robots, incapable of doing anything without an instruction from the programmer.

I believe we can go to God at any time with any subject, just like that boy could have gone to his father with questions he had. But God is not standing over us, issuing a stream of commands he expects us to obey. Rather, God wants us to grow and develop so that our relationship with him becomes one of friendship, not of simply obeying commands. This growth requires learning the skill of discernment.

Growing in Discernment

At least three voices compete for our attention as we seek to listen to God. One voice is the voice of our own thoughts. This voice may be wise or foolish, but the source is within our own selves. Another voice is the voice of evil spirits and the devil (called the tempter in 1 Thess 3:5), who also tempted Jesus (Matt 4:1). Thoughts of temptation come from this source, as do thoughts of condemnation. (See Rev 12:9–10.) Another voice is the voice of God. (See Heb 3:7.) Our task of discernment is to understand which voice we are listening to. Below, I give eight tests we can use to help us discern which voice we are listening to.

1. Is what I hear compatible with Scripture?

When we look at the ways God communicated with people as recorded in the Bible (dreams, visions, angelic appearances, thoughts in one's heart), we clearly see that God is not limited to only speaking to us through the pages of Scripture. Yet we must be very careful to remain rooted in Scripture. Some people, excited about the new things they are learning as they listen to God, gradually lose their moorings in Scripture and fall into error. If we receive a word that contradicts Scripture, then we must immediately throw out that word, whether it comes through thoughts received in our spirits or is given to us through a powerful angelic vision. "But even if we or an angel from heaven should preach a gospel other than the one we preached to you, let them be under God's curse!" (Gal 1:8).

Areas of special concern touch on Christ's death and resurrection from the dead (1 Cor 15:1–17), the sufficiency of his sacrifice to bring us into fellowship with God (Heb 9:14, 27–28; 1 John 4:10), and the deity of Christ (Col 2:9).[2] These are foundational areas where Satan will seek to bring us into confusion. But we sometimes ignore many other principles of Scripture to our own peril. A particular error is putting one's own revelation on par with Scripture or even above a principle of Scripture. Second

---

2. The early church did not have a problem comprehending the deity of Christ; rather they doubted that he was fully human (1 John 4:2). In our age the problem is reversed. Few doubt Jesus was human, but many do not believe in his divinity.

Pet 3:16 warns us of the danger that will come if we try to distort Scripture to suit our own situation.

Example

Amira is a young married woman. Formerly a devout Muslim, she became interested in Christianity through interacting with Christians online. After coming to Christ, she struggled in her marriage to a Muslim man and wished for an escape. She had many dreams about her husband cheating on her and concluded God was showing her that her husband was unfaithful, and therefore, she had no choice but to leave him. She did not find it easy to submit to the Scripture that says, "And if a woman has a husband who is not a believer and he is willing to live with her, she must not divorce him" (1 Cor 7:13).

2. Is my listening causing me to become like Jesus?

When Moses spoke with God on Mount Sinai, something happened to him. He was changed. "His face was radiant because he had spoken with the LORD" (Exod 34:29). In the same way, when we spend time in the Lord's presence, when we listen to Jesus, transformation ought to occur. "And we all, who with unveiled faces contemplate the Lord's glory, are being transformed into his image with ever-increasing glory, which comes from the Lord, who is the Spirit" (2 Cor 3:18).

Listening to Jesus brings transformation. If, over months and years of listening to Jesus we are not becoming like him, then something is seriously wrong. Although I am still very much a work in progress, as I look over the past few years of my own life, I can point to some areas of major transformation.

Example

We were on holiday in Greece and had rented a beautiful cottage on the island of Patmos. One morning, sitting in the sun, looking over the blue Aegean Sea, with no agenda, I was asking the Lord to speak to me. The response I heard in my heart was, "I love you." To be truthful, I had hoped for something a bit more earth-shattering than that. The next morning, I did the same thing. Somewhat to my disappointment, I heard the same response. It took me a while to understand that the Lord was addressing a wound deep within me. In the deepest places of my heart, much of my Christian life had been about seeking to earn God's favor by being good. I was never good enough to live up to my own expectations, and this was the driving force behind my perfectionist tendencies. The Lord was telling me that he loved me and that I didn't have to strive to earn his love. Over the years, as I have more deeply grasped God's love for me, I have found myself becoming more gracious in my response to others. Since I don't have to earn God's favor and acceptance, I can now more easily accept others with their faults.

3. What is the tone of the voice I hear?

The tone of a person's voice reveals much about the speaker. In my experience, God's voice is never harsh. Even in rebuke, he is kind and offers hope. God never belittles or mocks. God's voice is full of grace. Invariably after listening to him, I feel lighter. "God is love. Whoever lives in love lives in God, and God in them" (1 John 4:16).

If the voice we hear is harsh, critical either of us or of others, belittling, or mocking, then we need to be on guard. A voice that conveys no hope, that's filled with negativity, is not the Lord's. Examples of these include "you are stupid. You are ugly. You are an idiot." If the voice tells us to do things that are unloving to others, we are not on the right track. This doesn't mean that Jesus is soft. Sometimes the loving thing to do is very difficult. Yet Jesus is loving even when he corrects.

Example

Masud's parents came to faith in Jesus when he was young, and so Masud had the benefit of being raised in a Christian home. But Masud was not always an obedient child. During a time of inner healing prayer, we went through Masud's life from birth to adulthood. At several points, Masud related how he had become ensnared by pornography. At each of these junctures, we listened to what Jesus had to say. Each time, Jesus forgave Masud for his sin. Then we came to the point where Masud rushed into a marriage to a non-believer against his parents' wishes. Although Jesus showed him that the path ahead of him would be difficult and full of thorns, Jesus was never harsh or critical.

4. Does the voice I hear threaten me?

Fear is used to coerce a person to perform a particular action. In my experience, demonic forces coerce and instill fear, not God. A fear of extreme consequences if we do not obey is usually a sign we are not hearing the voice of Jesus. "There is no fear in love. But perfect love drives out fear, because fear has to do with punishment. The one who fears is not made perfect in love" (1 John 4:18). I am cautious about a commanding voice, especially when it is accompanied by fear. A continuous and insistent voice is also a warning sign that something is not right.

Example

As we saw in the example earlier in this chapter, Sanjoy lived in fear of disobedience, thinking that, if he disobeyed the voice he heard, he would commit the sin of blasphemy against the Holy Spirit. Anyone who is afraid he has committed the unforgivable sin, hasn't. If he had, he would have no interest in spiritual things. Instead, the person with this fear is being tormented by the voice of the devil and his minions.

5. Does the voice I hear lead me to greater humility?

The Bible gives frequent commands to be humble. Moses was extremely humble, and he heard God's voice very clearly. When we hear grand promises about becoming great or well-known or about preaching to thousands, we ought to be on our guard. God says, "I live in a high and holy place, but also with the one who is contrite and lowly in spirit" (Isa 57:15). We are told to imitate Jesus in his humility (Phil 2:5–8).

Example

I was upset over a recent conflict with an acquaintance. When I went to process the negative emotions with the Lord and my journal, I heard one word: apologize. I rebelled at the idea and thought, *If I apologize, she will think she is right.* But I did apologize, which had a restorative effect on our relationship. The Lord was leading me to take a step of humility.

6. Does the message I hear produce good fruit?

Different types of fruit come from listening to God. One form of fruit is events coming to pass as we understood God told us they would. Another form of fruit is the fruit of spiritual growth in our own lives. A greater level of faith, the courage to forgive, harshness replaced by kindness, or becoming less selfish, are some examples. (See the fruit of the Spirit enumerated in Gal 5:22–23.) All fruit, no matter the type, takes time to become visible. Often, we want to know immediately if we are hearing God correctly or not, but it will take some time before the fruit becomes evident.

Examples

Although he held a leadership position in a development project, Majeed used to struggle tremendously with making decisions. He worried about how the different parties affected by the decision would react. This commonly led to decidedly unhelpful actions, such as postponing decisions or trying to get others to make the difficult decisions for him. After learning how to listen to Jesus, Majeed's leadership changed dramatically. Majeed now makes decisions with confidence because he includes listening to God in his decision-making process. Good fruit came out of listening to Jesus.

Hasan tended to worry about many things: the permanency of his job, living as a Christian minority in a Muslim majority nation, and more. Frequently, he would come to a prayer time bound with tension. After learning how to listen to Jesus, he now worries a lot less. Again, good fruit came out of listening to Jesus.

I was sitting in an empty classroom studying for an exam in university. I had finally got into a decent rhythm and was absorbing the material. But as I studied, a pressurizing thought entered my mind that I must go and share the gospel with someone. I left my books in the classroom and looked for someone to talk to. I found a stranger in the nearby lounge area and began to share my faith with him. He disagreed with everything I had to say. I left that conversation with doubts in my own mind about some of my beliefs. When I went back to my books, I found I couldn't concentrate. The bad fruit that came out of that experience was evidence that the thought about sharing the gospel was not God's voice to me in that situation.

7. Do I have peace after my listening experience?

A sense of peace or its absence is one way to test that we have heard correctly and are walking in obedience to the Lord. However, when God asks us to do a difficult task, our powerful emotions of fear or embarrassment may overwhelm us and prevent us from sensing the Lord's peace in the moment. But if we obey, peace will eventually come.

Example

One day, our neighbor asked me if I could send $5,000 to her sister in Canada if she gave me the equivalent amount in local currency. I noted that the exchange rate she had used was favorable to me, so I went ahead with the transaction. During that period, although I was not skilled in listening to God's voice, I had been enjoying sweet fellowship with the Lord in my daily prayer times. But that evening, the sweet fellowship was not there, and I just did not have peace. I couldn't figure out why. Finally, I thought about the money and how I stood to make a tidy profit on the transaction. I really did not want to go back to my neighbor and return part of the money, but I sensed God wanted me to do just that. When I went to try to explain the matter, she didn't believe me and suspected I might keep the rest of her money and not send any to her relative. Talking to her was difficult and embarrassing and certainly did not fill me with peace in the moment, yet as I look back on the event, I have peace that I walked in obedience.

As we grow more accustomed to God's voice, we will begin to take note of a sense of the Lord's peace when we hear him. This sensitivity can take some time to learn.

8. Do mature Christians affirm that I have heard correctly?

The believing community plays a vital role in helping us test and confirm that we have correctly heard God's voice. When God called Paul and Barnabas, the whole church affirmed this was God's will by laying their hands on them and sending them out (Acts 13:1–3). When Paul saw the vision of the man from Macedonia, Paul's companions concluded together that God was leading them to that region (Acts 16:10). When Agabus predicted a famine, the believing community demonstrated through their actions that they were in agreement with what Agabus had said (Acts 11:28–30). When Agabus predicted Paul's imprisonment, the community again assented to the truth of what Agabus saw, even though they at first differed with Paul over the vision's meaning (Acts 21:10–14).

Applying the test of community can be confusing because the believing community as a whole is not always in tune with God's voice. Yet at least one or two godly people in our circle of Christians can almost always affirm that we are listening to God correctly. If you believe God is calling you to do something and you do not have the support of even one mature, godly individual, I would advise you to be extraordinarily cautious.

Riding a Bicycle

Who of us hasn't had a few accidents as we learned how to ride a bicycle? When I was a boy, I always seemed to have scabs on my knees due to one bicycle mishap or another. Mistakes are normal. We can't learn without making mistakes. If we seek to listen to God, we will make mistakes from time to time. When we or others make mistakes, we must not give up in discouragement and doubt the whole process of listening to God. Instead, we should be gracious to ourselves and then go back to the Lord in humility and ask him why we made a mistake.

Not every thought we receive is from the Lord. The Lord himself won't be offended if we test the thoughts we think are from him with the tests given in this chapter. In fact, the Bible commands us to test everything and hold on to the good (1 Thess 5:21).

After we have learned how to hear God's voice and test what we hear, we are in a position to help others listen to God. The last three chapters apply the lessons learned so far to helping others on their spiritual journeys. Before we get there, some people wish they could understand how the spiritual realm works. If that is you, turn to the next chapter.

Chapter 6

Understanding the Spiritual Realm

The Mechanics of a Gasoline Engine

WHEN I WAS TEN years old, our school held a science fair. Each student had to do a science project either alone or in partnership with a classmate. I found this a huge task. How could I put together a project like this? And moreover, I had no idea what subject to tackle. The teacher suggested I choose a topic that I didn't understand and learn about it. I didn't understand how a car engine worked. I knew that gasoline was dangerously flammable, and I had some conception of how a rocket engine worked, but I knew there was no rocket under the hood of my dad's car. I just couldn't figure out how burning gasoline could make the wheels turn. In the library, I found a book written at just my level that explained how gasoline exploded inside a cylinder, pushing a piston down. The piston attached to a connecting rod, which made the crankshaft rotate. By the end of the science fair, I had a pretty solid idea of how a gasoline engine worked.

The Mechanics of the Spiritual Realm

If we want to grow in understanding God's voice, it helps if we understand how he communicates with us. To understand this, we need to understand the spiritual realm and how it impacts the physical realm we are most familiar with. This chapter will help people who really like to understand how things work, but you don't need this chapter to listen to God.

I write this chapter with some trepidation. Some authors confidently make statements about what we cannot prove. I would rather write more tentatively and present what I believe to be true and invite you to verify what I have written with Scripture and your own experience. Some of the concepts in this chapter are clearly illustrated in Scripture. Other concepts, though not described in Scripture, give a plausible explanation to some of the phenomena we see. Several of these thoughts came out of insights from my own prayer experiences that I believe are compatible with what we see in Scripture. Let's talk about these concepts.

The Existence of the Spiritual Realm

There is a spiritual realm in addition to the physical realm with which we are familiar. The book of Ephesians refers to this realm as *epouranios*[1] which is often translated as "heavenly realms." Unfortunately, "heavenly" connotes one of two things to the modern reader. In some usages, it connotes the sky where birds fly or outer space where the stars exist. In other usages, the reader understands "heavenly" to describe the place where believers in Jesus will go after they die. Neither of these two connotations does justice to the word, as it is used in the book of Ephesians or in many other parts of the Bible.

So that we stop thinking about the place where birds fly or the place where we go after death, I will use the term "spiritual realm." In Eph 1:20, heavenly places, or the spiritual realm, is the place where God is, and Christ is seated at his right hand. Eph 2:6 tells us that we are also seated with Christ in the spiritual realm. Note that in English, this is translated in the present perfect tense, which means the action has been completed in the past with effects extending to the present time. Being seated with Christ is not merely some future hope; it is a present reality for believers in Jesus. We are now seated with Christ in the spiritual realm. In Eph 3:10, we find rulers and authorities in the spiritual realm to whom the wisdom of God needs to be made known, and finally, in Eph 6:12, we read that spiritual forces of evil in the spiritual realm impact us.

---

1. *Mickelson's*, s. v. "G2032 epouranios."

Interactions Between the Realms

What goes on in the spiritual realm affects what happens in the physical realm. "One day the angels came to present themselves before the LORD, and Satan also came with them. The LORD said to Satan, 'Where have you come from?' Satan answered the LORD, 'From roaming throughout the earth, going back and forth on it'" (Job 1:6–7). Not only could Satan converse with God in the spiritual realm, but we observe how he then went out and caused harm to Job in the physical realm. Similarly, when the prophet Micaiah was speaking to King Ahab, he reported that he saw a deceiving spirit speaking to the Lord. That deceiving spirit then went out from God's presence to "be a deceiving spirit in the mouths of all [Ahab's] prophets" (1 Kgs 22:19–23).

Not only does what goes on in the spiritual realm impact the physical, the reverse is also true. Beings in the physical realm can powerfully impact what goes on in the spiritual realm. Jesus told his disciples, "Truly I tell you, whatever you bind on earth will be bound in heaven, and whatever you loose on earth will be loosed in heaven" (Matt 18:18).

In the spiritual realm, God, Jesus, angels, and demons are present and active. What we refer to as heaven, the place where believers in Jesus go when they die, is in the spiritual realm. Angels and demons also inhabit parts of the spiritual realm and can affect us in the physical realm. The spiritual realm, although non-physical, is still very real. But where is it?

Increasing Our Dimensions

The spiritual realm is right here; it overlaps the physical realm. Whether we recognize it or not, we continually interact with the spiritual realm. Why then don't we perceive it? Why don't we engage with the spiritual realm with the same ease that we engage with the physical?

If we look at the physical and spiritual realms through the lens of two-dimensional and three-dimensional spaces, we discover what limits us. With this lens in place, let's assume the spiritual realm is a higher dimension of our universe than the physical realm.

Picture a two-dimensional universe filled with objects such as squares, circles, rectangles, and lines. Picture a friend at point X in this universe. He can travel left and right and up and down. (See Diagram 1.)

Diagram 1: A two-dimensional universe

Now let's envision a three-dimensional universe. Here, our friend at point X has more freedom of movement. He can move back and forth in addition to left and right and up and down. (See Diagram 2.)

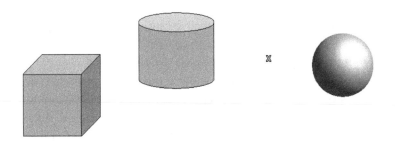

Diagram 2: A three-dimensional universe

Traveling between the dimensions

Suppose our two-dimensional friend has a vision. Suppose his mind is miraculously opened to comprehend the reality of a three-dimensional universe. He then reports, "In my vision, I saw something like a square, but it was fuller and far more complete than any of the squares we know. I then saw something they called a cylinder that had both the properties of a square and a circle, depending on the angle from which I viewed it. And the circle—oh, the circle!—it was beautiful beyond anything we have on earth."

Most of his two-dimensional friends would respond, "You are crazy! Your descriptions don't correspond with reality. No such universe exists.

How can a square be more complete than it already is? We only believe what we can see and touch."

Implications for us

I suspect the spiritual realm is a higher dimension of the universe in which we live and understand. Beings operating in the spiritual realm have greater freedom of movement than beings in the physical realm. Barriers like walls and gravity no longer apply to beings in the spiritual realm.

With his post-resurrection body, Jesus demonstrated this freedom of movement. Jesus had laid aside his ability to move in a higher dimension when he came to earth to be born as a baby (Phil 2:5–8). After the resurrection, however, he had no such restrictions. When Jesus met two disciples on the road to Emmaus, he stayed with them only until they recognized him. "When he was at the table with them, he took bread, gave thanks, broke it and began to give it to them. Then their eyes were opened and they recognized him, and he disappeared from their sight" (Luke 24:30–31).

From the disciples' perspective, he just disappeared. I suspect he simply traveled to a different location without the normal physical restraints we experience. The disciples, restricted to the physical, traveled on foot all the way back to Jerusalem. Fortunately for them, Jesus appeared there as well. "While they were still talking about this, Jesus himself stood among them and said to them, 'Peace be with you.' They were startled and frightened, thinking they saw a ghost. He said to them, 'Why are you troubled, and why do doubts rise in your minds? Look at my hands and my feet. It is I myself! Touch me and see; a ghost does not have flesh and bones, as you see I have'" (Luke 24:36–39).

Even though Jesus could freely interact in other dimensions, he abundantly proved he still had a physical body. We, with non-resurrected physical bodies, cannot yet bodily travel with the same freedom Jesus did. The way we access the spiritual realm with its freedom of movement is through our human spirits. Elisha demonstrated this. "When [Gehazi] went in and stood before his master, Elisha asked him, 'Where have you been, Gehazi?' 'Your servant didn't go anywhere,' Gehazi answered. But Elisha said to him, 'Was not my spirit with you when the man got down from his chariot to meet you? Is this the time to take money or to accept clothes—or olive groves and vineyards, or flocks and herds, or male and female slaves?'" (2 Kgs 5:25–26).

What are the practical results of all this, and how does this affect us? The spiritual realm is not simply some place in the sky. It is present here and now, everywhere we live, but since it is a higher dimension, most of the time, we are oblivious to it. Our human spirits inhabit the spiritual realm, whereas our human bodies are limited to the physical realm. When we get information from the spiritual realm, we are getting information from a higher dimension that we can only interpret using the symbols and language of the physical realm in which we live.

Being Human

With this understanding of the physical and spiritual realms as a background, what does it mean to be a human? The Bible makes it clear that humans are composed of a body, a soul, and a spirit (1 Thess 5:23), but much confusion abounds over what these terms mean.[2]

I sat down with my Bible one day, determined to understand the parts of a human. I wanted to know if the individual parts each had their own mind. Behind all my curiosity was whether it was possible to develop the spiritual part of our beings so that we could better commune with God. Not far into my study, I had an insight that made everything clear: We can understand the spiritual realm by drawing analogies with the physical realm.[3]

Often, people represent the tripartite nature of a person by drawing three concentric circles. The innermost circle represents the spirit; the middle circle, the soul; and the outermost circle, the body. But the next illustration is more helpful for me.

2. I realize others see this subject differently. Scholars such as Wayne Grudem see soul and spirit as essentially synonymous. Grudem, *Systematic Theology*, 472–7. I do not, however, feel Grudem's position is the best understanding of the biblical data. Contrary to Grudem, Franz Delitzsch adopts a trichotomous approach, as I do here. Delitzsch, *Biblical Psychology*, 103–19.

3. Much later, I discovered Paul also reasoned by analogy. "If there is a natural body, there is also a spiritual body" (1 Cor 15:44).

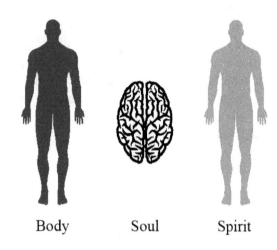

Body   Soul   Spirit

Diagram 3: A diagram of a human

Although I have drawn the three parts separately, the body, soul, and spirit overlap each other since they form a unified whole. Following the apostle Paul, we can more accurately say that the spirit and soul live in the body. "Now we know that if the earthly tent we live in is destroyed, we have a building from God, an eternal house in heaven, not built by human hands" (2 Cor 5:1).

The body inhabits the physical realm

The body is part of the physical realm and can receive input or perceive communication through its physical senses. It communicates in the physical realm by physical actions, such as speaking, writing, and touching. It can act on other objects or beings in the physical realm and be acted on by similar objects or beings in the physical realm.

The human spirit inhabits the spiritual realm

Every human has a spirit, and the human spirit is not the same as the Holy Spirit. The human spirit is part of the spiritual realm. It can receive communication through its spiritual senses and can also communicate with other spiritual beings in the spiritual realm. The actions of speaking and listening to God happen in the spiritual realm. The human spirit can also act on objects or other beings in the spiritual realm and can be acted on by those same objects or other beings in the spiritual realm. Communication with evil spirits happens in the spiritual realm. When we understand that the spiritual realm is analogous to the physical realm but a higher dimension, we can infer that the senses—taste, touch, sight, hearing, and smell—also exist in the spiritual realm but in a more complete manner.

The soul is the coordinator between the two

The soul is the coordinator between the body and the spirit. The soul contains the mind, the emotions, and the will. The soul has self-awareness. The soul contains the personality of the person. The soul is the executive function of the person—it takes what it receives from the body or the spirit and makes decisions. The soul can cause both the body and the spirit to act. The soul uses the body or the spirit to communicate. The soul can listen to or receive input from both the body and the spirit.

I like how the great preacher and missionary, Andrew Murray, puts it: "When God created man a living soul, that soul, as the seat and organ of his personality and consciousness, was linked on the one side, through the body, with the outer visible world, and on the other side, through the spirit, with the unseen and the divine. The soul had to decide whether it would yield itself to the spirit and by it to be linked with God and His will, or to the body and the solicitations of the visible."[4]

Each part of a human affects the other parts. Healthy thinking (what happens in the soul) can impact the body in positive ways. A wound in a person's spirit may lead to depressed thinking (effect on the soul) and lack of energy (effect on the body). Distinguishing between soul and spirit, between our own thoughts and thoughts that come to us from other beings in the spiritual realm, can be very difficult. (See Heb 4:12.)

What happens to the soul at death?

When a person's body dies, the soul departs, along with the human spirit, to either be with God or to face judgment. I believe a person retains memories

4. Murray, *Indwelling Spirit*, 32.

and personality after physical death. At death, a person appears to lose the limitations of the physical realm.

Numerous accounts exist of people who have survived serious accidents when their hearts stopped for a period of time. They were then resuscitated.[5] After resuscitation, they talk of interacting with angels and approaching heaven. When a person has such a near-death experience (NDE), their soul, along with their spirit, begins to leave their body. Upon resuscitation, their soul and spirit re-enter their body, but the soul retains memories of what happened as it was moving in the spiritual realm. In my opinion, however, we cannot accept all reports of NDEs uncritically. Some people possibly encounter deceptive spirits during such experiences and then bring back a report that everyone goes to heaven.

Spiritual but not Christian

When the Holy Spirit begins to inhabit a person at conversion, the Holy Spirit lives in or with the person's human spirit. When a person receives a new filling or baptism, their human spirit becomes more open to the work of the Holy Spirit.

Christians, however, are not the only people with access to the spiritual realm. Artists, writers, thinkers, and people who perceive things more deeply than others, even though not Christian, have at times tuned in to what is going on in their human spirit and thus accessed the spiritual realm. It is very dangerous to seek access to the spiritual realm through any other door than Jesus. Psychic phenomena are actions caused by the human spirit, some of which are aided by evil spirits.

Tuning in to the Spiritual Realm

Since God is spirit (John 4:24), his primary means of interacting with us is through our spirits. Assurance that we are God's children, for example, comes through this means (Rom 8:16). Although God has the power to speak to us through airwaves beating on our eardrums, I believe this is not his primary method of communication. He communicates most often through our human spirit, which our soul interprets as thoughts or pictures. The mind usually interprets these messages from the spiritual realm

5. Rawlings, *Beyond Death's Door*. See also Eby, *Caught Up Into Paradise*.

as its own. In fact, much of the time, we dismiss God's communication to us as our own random thoughts or imaginations. It is not that God doesn't speak to us; it is that we are not tuned in to him.

The first step in learning how to listen to God, therefore, is paying attention to what is going on in our spirits. Receiving messages through our spirits is different from analysis by using our minds. Analysis takes place in our souls. We listen to God in our spirits. If an answer to a question we ask God is an analysis of the situation, that is usually an indicator we have not heard from God; we are just processing our own thoughts. Analysis is good—we need to use analysis to judge what we hear. But analysis is not part of the listening process; it comes after.

The mind frequently interprets what is going on in the spiritual realm as its own thoughts or emotions. When an evil spirit communicates, we might receive thoughts like, *Life is hopeless; there is no point in trying. I just can't do anything right.* Or perhaps the predominant effect will be a generalized feeling of anxiety or fear—feelings we do not automatically recognize as coming from outside of us. Similarly, when the Holy Spirit speaks to us through our human spirits, we may interpret the message as our own thought. *Oh, I haven't called Anne in quite a while. I wonder how she is doing? Maybe I should call her today.* We can elevate thoughts from evil spirits as our own and believe them. We may perceive God's thoughts as our own and not attach sufficient importance to them.

Imagination Is the Door

We can use our imaginations as a door into the spiritual realm, as a means to help our minds tune in to what is going on in our spirits. I realize this will be a controversial idea for many people. Gen 6:5 says, "And God saw that the wickedness of man was great in the earth, and that every imagination of the thoughts of his heart was only evil continually" (KJV).

From childhood, many people have been taught that their imaginations are evil, or at best, they are fantasies that must be dismissed. The idea that imagination is evil is wrong for several reasons. First, Gen 6:5 is referring to people who had turned away from God. We cannot imply from this verse that the imagination of people who choose to follow God is always evil. Second, "imagination" can also be translated "mind," as in Isaiah 26:3 (KJV). If we replace "mind" with "imagination," this verse would read, "Thou wilt keep him in perfect peace, whose imagination is stayed on thee: because he trusteth in thee." In this case, mind or imagination is clearly good. Third, imagination is a critical part of our ability to think and conceptualize. Without imagination, nothing would be invented, and no complex problems would be solved.

Jesus expected us to use our imaginations. Every parable and story he told would cause his hearers to see pictures in their imaginations. Who can read Ps 23 without imagining sheep on a grassy hillside? It would be impossible to read the book of Revelation without invoking our imagination. Jesus says, "Here I am! I stand at the door and knock. If anyone hears my voice and opens the door, I will come in and eat with that person, and they with me" (Rev 3:20). These words evoke a picture. We can't read this verse without visualizing a house with a door and Jesus standing on the outside with his hand raised to knock.

Unfortunately, many people are afraid to use their imagination because they assume it is related to new age visualization techniques. New Agers use visualization techniques because they work. They do indeed bring people into contact with the spiritual realm. Opening our minds to the spiritual realm is not wrong in itself. It only becomes dangerous when we seek to do this apart from Jesus. If we do this, we are like the thieves and robbers who do not go in through the gate of the sheep pen. Jesus is the gate (John 10:7–9). Imagination functions like a door or window through which we can view our own thoughts, God's thoughts, and the activity of other spiritual beings. If you are afraid to look through this window, you may find it difficult to learn to hear God's voice.

As we saw in chapter 4, God himself taught the prophets to use their minds, their imaginations, to receive revelation from him.

> The word of the LORD came to me: "What do you see, Jeremiah?" "I see the branch of an almond tree," I replied. The LORD said to me, "You have seen correctly, for I am watching to see that my word is fulfilled." The word of the LORD came to me again: "What do you see?" "I see a pot that is boiling," I answered. "It is tilting toward us from the north." The LORD said to me, "From the north disaster will be poured out on all who live in the land." (Jer 1:11–14)

The word "see" can mean seeing something literally or figuratively.[6] Here, we observe God training Jeremiah to see spiritually. God either took a real physical object in front of Jeremiah and spoke to him through that

6. *Mickelson's*, s. v. "H7200 ra'ah."

76

object, or God accessed an object in Jeremiah's mind. In both cases, Jeremiah used the imagination or the capability of the mind to visualize.

In conclusion, there are two realms. The spiritual realm can be understood as a higher dimension that contains the physical realm but adds complexity and fullness to it. As humans, we are composed of a body, a soul, and a spirit. Our body lives and interacts in the physical realm, whereas our spirit lives and interacts in the spiritual realm. Since God is spirit, he will communicate with us primarily through our human spirit. Our soul is the coordinating mechanism between our bodies and our spirits. Most of the time, our souls are preoccupied with what is going on in the physical realm and consequently, we miss out on what God is communicating. If we want to hear God's voice, we will find it helpful to use our imagination as the door through which we enter into what God is doing in the spiritual realm. We will see practical examples of this in the next three chapters.

Chapter 7

Listening in Discipleship

Discipleship or Meeting Jesus?

I HAD TRAVELED TO another ministry area and was staying with friends. Fazil, mentioned earlier in the book, came over to visit. When we have the chance, Fazil and I talk about spiritual matters, read Scripture together, and pray. This time as we talked, Fazil expressed the deep pain he felt over the shallowness of many believers in Jesus. Relying on my own experience, I could have said many things to try and encourage my friend to persevere. Or I could have advised him to leave these shallow people and start afresh with others.

By this point in my journey, I had come to understand that it would be far more effective for Fazil to listen to Jesus's voice than my own wisdom. Since I knew I would only have about thirty minutes of uninterrupted time with him, I wanted to get to core matters quickly. With very little preamble, I led him in a listening session. As we quieted our hearts and focused on Jesus, Fazil saw himself bowed down before Jesus, expressing the burden on his heart. Jesus put one hand on the top of his head and with the other lifted his chin. Then Jesus spoke to his heart. "This is my work." The tears running down Fazil's face showed me that Jesus had touched the core issue. The result was far more effective than what I could have accomplished. It also took much less time.

Failed Discipleship Programs

If the end goal is becoming like Jesus, most discipleship programs do not work. They don't work because they miss a crucial element. Some programs focus on imparting right beliefs—knowledge transfer. The discipler teaches the basics of the faith, such as sin, salvation, sanctification, and an overview of the Bible. Growing in knowledge, however important, does not in itself result in transformation. Some Christians know a lot of Biblical doctrine but are not like Jesus.

Other discipleship programs focus on discipleship practices—developing disciplines of daily Bible reading, prayer, church attendance, Bible memorization, tithing, and sharing one's faith. While spiritual disciplines are necessary for almost everyone, discipleship through disciplines has serious limitations. Here, discipleship becomes all about performance. The disciple hears the subtle message that if he performs according to certain standards, he will be loved and accepted by God.

New believers, eager to be fed and trained, make significant strides through knowledge-based and practice-based discipleship programs, but these alone are not sufficient to bring about the deep transformation needed in their lives. And what about older believers, those who have been believers for years, those who have tried various methods and given up along the way? Many mature believers hesitate to give discipleship another shot.

Starting Discipleship Relationships

"Do you want to meet with me once every two weeks so that I can teach you how to understand the Bible and grow in your faith?" A new believer, full of enthusiasm, might take me up on this offer, but people who have been believers for years feel as if they already understand the Bible. And what would I teach? If discipleship means coming up with a new, mentally stimulating Bible study every week or two, I begin to feel overwhelmed. I have an extremely demanding day job. Planning Bible studies takes a lot of effort. Is there a better method?

Jesus as the Discipler

I am convinced that the missing piece is an ongoing, live meeting with Jesus. Meeting Jesus brings transformation. As people learn to listen to Jesus and walk in obedience to him, their lives are changed. Jesus made disciples by spending time with people in a practical, hands-on way. He talked to them about their personal lives. He answered their questions. He explained what went wrong when a situation didn't work out. He gave tasks and then followed up with them on how things went. He gave responsibility.

What if it were possible to teach people how to listen to Jesus themselves? What if they could learn how to bring their questions to him and hear his answers? What if Jesus himself wanted to give people discipleship tasks and then follow up to see how those tasks went? What if he was in charge of choosing the areas in the disciple's life that needed to be changed? In short, what if Jesus himself was the primary discipler? If that were so, my primary role would be helping the disciple to establish his relationship with Jesus and then checking in on a regular basis to make sure the disciple was staying in conversation with Jesus.

I am not suggesting we ignore Bible study and spiritual practices. By no means! I am simply suggesting that without a conversational relationship with Jesus, these practices not only become dull and lifeless, they often fail to produce deep change.

The Choosing of the Six:
Embarking on a Discipling Journey

I had been growing in my own experience of listening to Jesus and gradually became convinced that others could be taught the skill of listening to Jesus. What if a discipleship program could be formed around this concept? Would it work? I was keen to find out.

I decided that my new discipleship syllabus should be very simple—it only had three points: First, I would try to teach the person how to listen to Jesus. Then, I would emphasize the importance of obedience to what Jesus said. Finally, I would encourage the disciple to make other disciples following the same pattern.

I started looking for people whom I could invite into this kind of relationship. Hasan was a great candidate. I was already meeting with him from time to time, and the Lord seemed to be blessing that relationship. I was also thinking about Shahin but wasn't sure if he was the right choice. At that time, the house church met on Friday afternoons. Before one weekly worship service, I told the Lord, if Shahin comes to church today, I will invite him into a discipling relationship.

He came, and during the prayer time, he shared. "I wasn't intending to come to church this afternoon because I had a program in the north suburb this morning. But someone gave me a ride back into town, and so here I am." I took this as a clear sign from the Lord.

There were others. Tufayel came over one evening because he wanted my physiotherapist wife to treat his back pain. After the treatment time, while Ingrid was preparing a snack, I chatted with Tufayel about listening to Jesus. Although he had been a believer from childhood, at this point in his life, his relationship with Jesus had become quite distant. This conversation piqued his curiosity, and so he arranged a time when he could come and talk more. On the appointed day, he came with his wife. Both experienced the Lord's presence and voice in a powerful way that evening.

Let's look at one person's discipleship journey.

A Discipleship Journey

Hasan, whom I had known for about eleven years, was my test case. He would come over to vent his frustrations, ask questions about the Bible, and pray. Could I teach him to listen to Jesus, and could this practice be incorporated into a discipling relationship? In our first meeting on this new journey, I explained the concept of listening to God, and we began to practice together.

I am always excluded

In our second meeting, Hasan came with an issue weighing heavily on his mind. The source of his troubles was the young adults' group that he was a part of at his church. Hasan's family used to be Muslim, but they now followed Jesus. Everyone else in the church group was raised in a traditional Christian family. Hasan didn't think like them and felt inferior. What would be considered good-natured teasing by others bothered Hasan. As we quieted our hearts and listened, Hasan received three thoughts: "You are different, but you are not bad. It is not always about whether you are enjoying the meeting. You are not always excluded."

As we continued to listen, deeper revelation came. Hasan explained what the Lord was showing him. "I am excluded because I want to be excluded. I don't want to do what is required to build relationships. Building relationships means that I have to step outside my comfort zone. Even before going to a meeting, I am afraid of being excluded."

Then Jesus gave the solution. "Don't fear. Have a positive attitude. Go with a giving mind."

By the third meeting, Hasan had concluded that he needed to spend more time with the Lord. I discovered that I no longer had to urge people to pray, read their Bible, and spend time in personal devotions. Jesus tells that directly to the listener, often in the very first meeting.

Oh no, Lord, I don't want to talk about that

By the time the fourth meeting came around, I decided to try something different. In my devotions that morning, I thought, *I am teaching others how to listen to God, I should try to listen to God myself for the person I am discipling.* I quieted my heart and asked the Lord if he had anything to say about Hasan. Immediately a sentence popped into my mind. *He is thinking about marriage.* My brain immediately revolted. *No, Lord, I don't want to talk about that. He is single and has a good job. Of course he wants to get married. And I am probably just making this up anyway.* Then I thought, *I asked God to speak to me. Maybe I should have a little bit of faith and take this as a word from the Lord.* So I asked if the Lord had anything else to say about marriage. The answer came. *Walk with him in this.* That answer turned out to be far truer than I expected.

Hasan came over about an hour later, and after a bit of chitchat, I asked, "Are you thinking about marriage?"

He replied, "Not really. I'm only thinking about this ten percent." I had assumed that if God said that he was thinking about marriage, it would be the biggest issue on his mind. Before I could start feeling depressed about making what I thought was a mistake, Hasan continued. "But all my relatives are pressuring me to get married." Hasan went on to explain that he didn't think he was qualified to lead a family because his Bible knowledge was not that great and he was not spiritually mature enough.

Realizing that I hadn't been totally wrong, I suggested we ask Jesus what he had to say about this. I then led him in a reflective prayer. By starting a listening time with a reflection on Jesus, many people can engage easily with God and hear his voice. I told him to see himself in a beautiful place and then look around for where Jesus was. Then I waited.

After Hasan opened his eyes, he seemed a bit embarrassed to share what had happened. Hasan's experience was totally different from the reflective prayer I started with. Hasan saw himself sitting at his desk in his office at the bank. A customer walked up. Hasan looked up in surprise and said, "Oh Jesus, you are here." Jesus then asked him, "What do you think about marriage?" Hasan replied, "I am just thinking about you. All I want is you." Jesus responded, "Don't keep your eyes completely closed." And then the vision ended.

As we talked about this, I asked Hasan to clarify what this vision meant to him practically. Hasan answered that when others point out a girl to him, he shouldn't immediately say no.

This is getting scary

Over the following months, God continued to speak to Hasan. He heard from God about family issues he was facing, about office politics at his workplace, and about his worries concerning his own reputation. His thoughts had also begun to move toward marriage. One day, Hasan told me he was wondering if he should develop a relationship with a girl named Meem. As he listened, God showed him the face of another girl and said, "Not Meem but Shumi." I felt very uncomfortable about this. It seemed dangerous to believe that God had shown him someone to marry before a relationship had even started. For Hasan, anyway, this was totally impossible. Shumi was already in a relationship with a guy whom Hasan felt was better placed than he. This guy was working abroad and was tall and good-looking. I decided to leave this matter in God's hands. If God had truly spoken, it would come to pass.

Painful memories

Several years earlier, while a student in university, Hasan used to engage in informal religious debates with Muslim students, seeking to point out the flaws in their belief system. One day, Hasan had been arguing points of religion with members of a militant group. Since Hasan is a Muslim name, it wasn't clear to the debaters that Hasan was a Christian. To them, he was merely a liberal Muslim arguing with conservatives. At one point in the conversation, they accused him of being a Christian and in fear, Hasan denied it. Since that time, Hasan had been haunted by the fact that he had denied his faith and maybe lost his salvation. As we listened to the Lord on this subject, Jesus said to Hasan, "Look, I am not an unloving God. I understand your weakness. From that time on, you have grown from strength to strength." Since that day, Hasan has never again expressed doubt about his salvation to me.

While still on the subject of painful memories, I suggested to Hasan that he needed to process some painful memories regarding his mother as a step toward preparing for marriage. Hasan responded, "There are a lot. If I get married, I will not be able to live at home." It was two months before the opportunity to process these memories came.

Getting to the root

One day, a couple of months later, I told Hasan that I saw a pattern of certain issues repeating themselves in his life. These were things like comparing himself with others his age who had achieved more success, a sense of inferiority, anger toward his mother, a bleak outlook on life, and lots of fears. Many times, we had prayed through these issues and, after an hour together, Hasan's outlook dramatically improved. Then, several weeks later, he struggled with the same issues again. I wondered if we were only dealing with symptoms and not attending to the deeper wounds buried in Hasan's heart. I suggested we do some inner healing work—processing painful childhood memories that cause dysfunction in adulthood. (I address inner healing more fully in the next chapter.)

Inferiority

As we worked through childhood memories, one memory from when Hasan was about age ten turned out to be particularly significant. Hasan's mother had collected him from school. Hasan saw the other students eating out at fast-food restaurants, so Hasan asked his mother to take him out too. She replied, "We are not like them. When they eat burgers, we eat bread. When they drink coke, we drink water." Hasan felt as if they were very, very low in society and that others were very, very high. This was one of the points when the seeds of inferiority were sown—seeds that grew up to be great trees, producing evil fruit in later life.

As Hasan entered that childhood memory with Jesus, he heard Jesus say, "My society is different from the society around you." Hasan didn't understand, so he asked for more explanation. Again, Jesus spoke. "My society means those who belong to me." These simple words brought courage to Hasan's heart. I then led Hasan in the step of forgiving his mother who had, albeit unknowingly, caused harm in his life. Up to this point, Hasan's comments about his mother had been almost universally negative.

The fruit of this exercise was not long in coming. One of the most striking changes was Hasan's attitude toward his mother. A couple of weeks after this event, there was a church picnic. Hasan invited his mother (who did not attend that church) and sister to come along.

A few months later, Hasan married Shumi, the girl whose face the Lord had shown him less than a year earlier. And this union is turning out to be a happy one. According to local custom, Hasan is living with his parents, something he was sure would be impossible. The relationship between a mother-in-law and a daughter-in-law is frequently filled with strife in this culture, but Hasan's wife gets along well with Hasan's mother. There has been great healing in that family.

Transformation occurred

Over a period of less than two years, Hasan went from being a shy person, angry at his mother, not wanting to get married, full of deep inferiority, and with lots of doubts, to a place where he was willing to hold on to what God had shown him despite difficult circumstances. Hasan has grown in confidence. His relationship with his mother has radically shifted. Now he is happily married and continuing to grow in his walk with God. More importantly, he has a much deeper understanding of God's love for him.

Discipleship Is Easy

If discipleship depends on my ability to create interesting content that keeps people engaged from meeting to meeting, then discipleship is hard. If discipleship depends on knowing how to solve the problems of my disciples, then discipleship is hard. If discipleship depends on my ability to motivate a person to behave a certain way and do certain activities, such as evangelism, daily prayer, and Bible study, then discipleship is hard.

But if discipleship is showing people how they can live a life in conversation with Jesus, then discipleship is easy. I am no longer responsible to bring about change. I am no longer responsible to produce right behavior.

That is Jesus's job. My job is merely to introduce the person to a conversational relationship with Jesus and then check in from time to time to make sure the relationship is still active.

My method is simple. In the first meeting, I share from Scripture how God speaks to people. There are many passages to choose from on this subject:

- The shepherd calls his sheep by name on a daily basis (John 10:3–5).

- Jesus calls us friends (John 15:14). It is hard to conceive of being friends with someone and not talking to that person. In the same passage, we are taught to remain in Jesus (John 15:5–6). Does not being in such close connection with Jesus imply mutual communication?

- Jesus spoke of the Counselor, the Holy Spirit who would come. The Counselor communicates (John 16:5–15).

- Both the psalmist (Ps 115:4–7) and Paul (1 Cor 12:2) contrasted our God with mute idols. The clear message is that God is not mute.

- Several of the spiritual gifts mentioned by Paul require receiving God's communication to operate (1 Cor 12:8; 14:6).

- Eating with Jesus implies deep conversation (Rev 3:20).

- For those preferring Old Testament narratives, I like to look at Samuel's life. He needed instruction from Eli at the beginning (1 Sam 3:1–10). Then he went on to hear God's voice in his heart (1 Sam 16:1–13).

After looking at Scripture, I lead in a listening session. Normally, I encourage the person to ask Jesus what he thinks of them. Instead of hearing a voice of judgment, most people hear God's voice of tenderness and compassion. Frequently, the person expresses the desire to spend more time with the Lord in prayer and Bible reading. In the next meeting, I follow up with how their listening went since we last met. I answer questions and try to deal with doubt or confusion that a person faces.

Invariably, people experience some level of doubt. I suspect doubt is one of Satan's primary tools to distract people from a practice that will result in a deep transformation of their lives if they continue in it. At this stage, they need a lot of encouragement. I tell people that they can always check in with me if they are unsure that what they are hearing is correct. I show them how they can test what they hear.

After the person becomes comfortable with the practice of listening, I bring up the concept of inner healing. Sometimes wrong attitudes and beliefs stifle a person's spiritual growth. I show the person how he can start in a positive memory of being with Jesus and then hold Jesus's hand and walk into a difficult memory. Some people are helped by going through a systematic process, such as that outlined in Charles Kraft's *Two Hours to Freedom*. For others, simply using Karl Lehman's *Immanuel Approach* with specific painful memories is sufficient. (See the next chapter for more on inner healing.)

The goal is to make listening and obeying a life practice. One key is practicing frequently, both on their own and with their discipler. Another key is being obedient to what God tells them. This will bring change and excitement into their walk with God.

What I've Learned in the Process

I chose six people to disciple and used a three-point syllabus of learning to listen to God, obeying what he says, and teaching others to do the same. This began my most fruitful period of ministry in South Asia over a twenty-year period. I learned several things in this process.

Desire to spend more time with the Lord

The almost invariable response after hearing the Lord speak for the first time was "I need to spend more time with the Lord." This was a complete change from my previous model, where I felt like I had to persuade people to engage in spiritual disciplines. Now I didn't have to tell them; Jesus himself told them, and his words carried a lot more weight than mine did.

Character change

The Lord's voice brings character change. I watched how the Lord addressed fears in the hearts of my disciples. Many times, the Lord showed them a different point of view, a new perspective that helped free them from entrenched thinking patterns. The Lord showed new steps they could take in situations they faced. Several times, God spoke, and then a few weeks later, we saw the event come to pass as God had said, resulting in greatly strengthened faith. In some cases, God brought healing to deep wounds that had been buried for many years. The disciples forgave those who had hurt them. The Lord's voice brought healing to these wounds, not my explaining and reasoning.

Disappointments

Not everyone continued in the discipling relationship. Tufayel and his wife didn't come back after a powerful first session together, even though the Lord touched them both deeply. Another young man met with me for nine months. The Lord spoke to him almost every time we met. As I look over my notes from the listening sessions, I can see his progression and spiritual growth. I got to understand the deeply loving heart of Jesus as I listened to this young man relate how Jesus had spoken to him. He stopped coming after he revealed a deeply personal matter that was affecting his life direction. Maybe he was too afraid to face this issue.

With another person, I pushed a little bit too hard into personal areas where I thought transformation needed to happen. We never met again, and I painfully learned the importance of waiting until the Lord brings up the issues he wants to deal with.

Starting the relationship is easy

From the beginning, I learned that starting this kind of discipling relationship is easy. If you ask someone to commit to a series of Bible studies with you, most of the time you tend to get a lukewarm reception; people are busy. But if you say to someone, "I am really excited about how we can listen to what God is saying to us personally. Do you want to learn?" the response is almost always positive. Even a skeptic is at least curious enough to meet once. After they hear God's voice for the first time, they usually want to keep meeting.

Multiplication

The method I use is highly transferable. Once you gain practice in listening to Jesus yourself, you can teach others to do the same. I am very ambitious and optimistic, so I hoped that recursive disciple-making would result in a movement. Since I was starting my new discipleship program with people who were already believers, I thought that within six months, they would grasp the concepts and want to teach others. After six months passed, my disciples were still meeting with me regularly but were not confident enough to pass what they were learning on to someone else. After one and a half years, one person has taught someone else, and another has brought his brother to be taught. If Jesus's disciples needed to spend time with him 24/7 for three years before they began to change the world, maybe my six-month time frame was a little overzealous.

Being Like Jesus

Hasan came over one morning, and we had a great time together. The Lord spoke to him about several issues that were on his mind. Then he went home and listened to the Lord on his own. The Lord told him to phone his colleague Ajit and tell him that God loves him. That sparked within Ajit a desire to learn how to listen to the Lord as well.

Discipleship is being, not just knowing or even doing. It is the formation of a person from spiritual babyhood to adulthood under the care of a more mature spiritual person. The good news is that this is easy if we let Jesus be the primary discipler. We do not have to be spiritual giants in order to disciple others. We do not need to have years of Bible training. We just need to teach people how to listen to Jesus.

One stage in the discipleship journey is dealing with our buried hurts and wounds. We will look at this in the next chapter.

Chapter 8

Listening and Inner Healing

A Crying Five-Year-Old

ETCHED IN HER MIND was the picture of a five-year-old girl, crying inconsolably. Taken away from her parents and all that was familiar, she was going to a hostel, a strange place with strange people.[1] What caused Shumi, a twenty-five-year-old happily married woman with a good education and a decent job, to return to this childhood memory?

Shumi had been telling my wife, Ingrid, and me how several families were dependent on the income of her and her husband. She was convinced that both she and her husband had to work to support their relatives. Ingrid asked, "Where does the fear come from? What is the root?"

We told Shumi to quiet her heart and focus on Jesus. We wanted her to ask Jesus about the source of her fear of financial lack. But Shumi couldn't focus. Questions such as, "Has someone cursed me?" and "Has my behavior toward others been good enough?" swirled in her mind. The name of an abusive boyfriend kept coming to her thoughts. While Shumi's mind was wandering, Ingrid was tuning in to the Lord. After the prayer time, Ingrid said, "The word I heard was 'abandonment.'"

---

1. In South Asia there are numerous group homes for children, sometimes called orphanages or hostels. Often, children are sent to these homes for economic reasons, even though one or both parents are still living. Many hostels are run by Christian organizations with the intention that the children will be raised in a Christian environment, have access to a solid education, and be saved from the evils of child marriage. Despite the noble efforts of these organizations, leaving one's parents at a young age can cause lasting problems that continue even after the child reaches adulthood.

Shumi replied, "I've always felt this way. Only I was sent away to live in a hostel while my siblings stayed at home. Even today, I still don't have a solid relationship with my parents." Illustrating the unconscious rejection she felt, Shumi continued, "My father cried when I was born and he learned that I was a girl."

God had evidently led us to a traumatic memory, and the trauma was making it hard for Shumi to listen to Jesus. This called for an inner healing prayer session. I asked Shumi to re-enter her memory of crying inconsolably while she was being taken from her parents. "Look around in that memory," I said. "Where is Jesus?"

After a period of silence, she replied, "He is planning a better future for me." This was indeed true. Shumi had turned out to be an excellent student. She was a member of a strong church and loved the Lord. Now she was married to a man who cared for her deeply. She would not have had these opportunities if she had been raised in her parents' poverty.

Then Jesus spoke to her heart, "Are you better off or worse because of the hostel?" Shumi remained silent. After her self-pity, she was ashamed to admit she was better off due to living in the hostel. Shumi continued the conversation that was going on in her heart. "Why do these fears come?" she asked. "Because you are not depending on me," came the answer. As the session ended, Shumi expressed her desire to connect more deeply with the Lord. The lightness in her countenance bore testimony to the significance of what had happened in her heart. The cloud of abandonment had lifted.

Inner Healing Does Not Have to Be Difficult

In the church in the West, we typically refer people who have experienced difficult events to professional counselors. In many cases, that is the most appropriate thing to do. Yet some people will never pluck up the courage to make an appointment with a counselor. Some do not have the finances. In contexts like South Asia, it may be very difficult to even find a counselor who understands the local language and culture and is available to minister. Others have experienced only minor trauma. They do not consider their issues significant enough to bring to a counselor, yet their issues impact their relationships with God and others around them.

I am convinced that the body of Christ ought to be equipped to bring healing to its members. The four-step process I present in this chapter works for most people after they have grasped the basics of listening to

Jesus's voice. A person can begin by practicing on himself and then move on to helping others after he experiences healing in his own life. Let's take the initial steps to help our hurting brothers and sisters find healing and then refer those who really need it to the professionals.

Background Concepts

Before we jump into a simple process for leading a person in inner healing, we need to understand some background concepts.

Our past affects our present

Many of our fears and dysfunctions in adulthood stem from wounds we have sustained in childhood. These wounds continue to affect our lives in adulthood, but most of the time we are oblivious as to the source. Dr. Terry Wardle, the president of Healing Care Ministries, put it this way.

> You cannot simply forget the past. And often the past won't stay in the past. The past becomes very active in the present. When we've experienced unresolved emotional wounding from the past, it begins to leak into the way we view ourselves, the way we view God, the way we view other people, and even the way we begin to respond to the events of our lives. The unresolved past can have a tremendous negative impact on us when we carry it into the future.[2]

If we want to experience inner healing in the present, then we need to be willing to revisit our past with Jesus.

There is a difference between pain and trauma

During the birth of my eldest sibling, the doctor said to my mother, "Don't worry; the next one will be easier."

Mom groaned in reply, "There isn't going to be another one." I am thankful that the pain of that event lessened in her mind and she went on to bear three more children. Childbirth is extraordinarily painful, but

---

2. https://hcmi.kartra.com/videopage/whyisthepastalwayspresent, accessed on September 6, 2020. Terry Wardle is the author of numerous books including *Some Kind of Crazy* (2019), *Identity Matters* (2017), and *Healing Care, Healing Prayer* (2003).

not necessarily traumatic. Most of the time, the mother is surrounded by a caring community. After the birth, joy comes as a new member is added to the family. The pain has reason and meaning, so it does not usually result in longstanding trauma. We have all faced painful experiences in our lives, but not all painful events are traumatic.[3]

Trauma, on the other hand, is unprocessed pain. Unprocessed pain becomes toxic. Even relatively small pains, such as being the last one chosen to be on a team at recess, or not being allowed to go to a childhood party, can become toxic if they are not properly processed. I believe most people have some level of unprocessed pain in their lives. For some, the amount of pain is relatively small, and so the effects are small. For others, the amount of toxicity is high and causes misery both to them and those around them.

Example: The Grade Two Teacher

Allyson was practicing listening to Jesus. Her initial question was "Jesus, what thinking do I need to change in order to be in agreement with you?" I felt this was a pretty big question to start with and so advised her to begin her listening time by just being with Jesus and hearing his words of affirmation. As I coached her on what questions she could ask Jesus, her conversation went something like this:

Allyson: What do you like about me?

The first thought Allyson received in response to this question was the idea of being scolded for having her own thoughts. She put this thought aside and tried to hear the voice of Jesus.

Jesus: You are mine.

Allyson: This answer makes me feel as if there is no good quality in me.

Jesus: God doesn't make mistakes. He can help you change.

Although I am not a professional counselor, this part of the conversation should have been sufficient to tell me Allyson probably had a buried issue that needed processing. The great thing about listening to Jesus is that it doesn't depend on my skills. What I needed to do here was help Allyson continue the conversation with Jesus, and Jesus himself would eventually

3. For more information on this topic, see Lehman, *Immanuel Approach*, 12–15.

help Allyson to see the issue she needed to process. I continued to suggest questions that Allyson could ask Jesus:

Allyson:	What step can I take to hear you better?
Jesus:	Actually believe that you are worthy of being spoken to.
Allyson:	Where does the sense of unworthiness come from?
Jesus:	Repeated failures.

I wasn't completely sure that Allyson had correctly grasped the heart of Jesus here, but we continued to practice asking questions and listening to the answers.

Allyson:	What do you say about my failures?
Jesus:	I make all things new.
Neil:	Do you believe this?
Allyson:	I believe it for other people.

Allyson's hesitation to believe that God would make all things new for her made me suspect she needed inner healing in an area of her life. A skilled counselor could probably have figured that out much earlier, but this process is not about being an awesome counselor; it is about helping a person hear Jesus's voice and allowing him to speak into the situation. At this point, I transitioned to inner healing prayer. I briefly explained the process and told Allyson to ask Jesus to show her the first memory where this sense of unworthiness came in. Allyson related a memory of her verbally abusive grade two teacher. The teacher's behavior reinforced the verbal abuse of an older sibling.

Neil:	Walk with Jesus into this memory and ask him what he has to say.
Jesus:	She is not me.

Allyson had taken on the verbal abuse of others and attributed it to what God thought of her. As we continued to talk, Allyson told me she had received the answer to her original question. The thinking she needed to change to be in agreement with Jesus was the thinking that she is worthless.

To get healing in the present, we have to deal with the traumatic memories in the past

Allyson had experienced verbal abuse in childhood, which resulted in persistent feelings of unworthiness in adulthood. Many people struggle with painful root memories that color the way we look at life. We can ask Jesus to guide us to root memories that we need to deal with. Sometimes the root memory seems like a minor issue (who hasn't had at least one nasty teacher?), and we may be tempted to dismiss it. Rather than dismiss it, we should invite Jesus into that memory as Allyson did.

Jesus's words bring healing

Jesus's words bring another perspective to the situation. Jesus showed Allyson that the harsh words of her teacher were not his words. When Jesus speaks, healing comes.

Finding a Memory

To do inner healing, you have to have a difficult memory to work with. Sometimes this memory has already surfaced in conversation. Sometimes you merely suspect the presence of painful memories because of the wrong thinking expressed. Like Allyson did, you can ask Jesus to guide you to a root memory. A helpful way to put it is "Jesus, please show me the first instance (or an early instance) where this kind of thinking or feeling occurred." For Allyson that root memory was of an event that occurred when she was seven and in grade two.

A Simple Process

Step 1: Start in a positive memory

Thinking about painful memories stirs up emotions which, in turn, make it more difficult to communicate effectively. For this reason, the person you are helping should start in a positive memory.[4] I suggest that the person I am working with think back to a time when God was especially close to

---

4. Lehman, *Immanuel Approach*, 82.

him, such as a time of deep worship or when he was in great difficulty and cried out to God and God responded by helping him. Any positive memory works. When the person has chosen a positive memory, I invite him to re-enter it. I invite him to see the events, see the surroundings, and feel the emotions.

When the person is in the memory, I ask, "Where is Jesus?" We know that since Jesus is God, he is everywhere and always present. Picturing Jesus there with him prepares the person to listen to Jesus's voice. Sometimes he can easily picture Jesus there with him. Sometimes he has a general awareness of the presence of God. When in the positive memory, I ask him to observe how Jesus interacts with him. How does Jesus greet him? How does he see himself responding to Jesus's greeting?

Step 2: Go with Jesus into the painful memory

After the person has interacted with Jesus in the positive memory, I coach him to walk with Jesus into the painful memory. As in the positive memory, I invite him to look around and notice who is there, what is going on, and what feelings he is experiencing, all the while, holding onto Jesus's hand or simply being aware of his presence.

Step 3: Listen to Jesus's voice in the painful memory

When he is with Jesus in the painful memory, I tell him to ask Jesus what he has to say. The words of Jesus in the painful memory bring a change in perspective, resulting in inner healing. If I ever get stuck because the person I am working with struggles to interact with Jesus in the painful memory, I lead him back to the positive memory and end the session there. We will always have another opportunity, or in some cases, we can refer the person to a professional counselor.

Step 4: Share what happened

Sharing what happened is a critical part of the process. Verbalizing the experience both makes it more real and cements the interaction in his mind. If this is not done, the experience quickly fades, or the person does not grasp the significance of what just happened.

The beauty of this method of inner healing is that it does not depend on your spiritual gifts or counseling skills. All you are doing is facilitating a direct connection with Jesus for the person you are helping. Your main role is to make an introduction to Jesus and oversee the conversation. If the person you are helping gets stuck, you can either lead him back to a positive memory with Jesus or suggest an alternative question for him to ask Jesus.

Difficulties

Hearing wrongly

In my experience, the person rarely hears something that is obviously wrong. If that does happen, it is usually because of some distortion in his thinking that has not yet been corrected. Many times, simply continuing the conversation allows Jesus to gently correct the person's thinking.

Visualizing versus awareness

For most people, picturing or visualizing Jesus works really well and leads to some very special interactions. Others speak of an awareness of God's presence around them but do not see Jesus in their mind's eye. We should not require the person to visualize. An awareness of God's presence is enough to carry on a conversation.

Not hearing anything

If the person is not accustomed to listening to Jesus, he may say that he cannot hear his voice. In that case I often ask, "What do you think Jesus would say in this situation?" This simple question releases the person from the pressure of trying to get the words exactly right, enabling him to tune in to what Jesus is saying to him in his heart.

Example: Playing with friends

I was beginning an inner healing prayer session with Kalpona. As we started, I asked her to find a positive memory. She saw herself playing with two of her friends:

"What is God saying as he looks down on you playing together?" I asked.

"I don't know."

"What do you think God is thinking?"

"He is happy."

Kalpona was reliving the event of being beaten by her mother:

I asked, "What is God saying to you in that situation?"

"I don't know."

"What do you think God would say in that situation?"

"It hurts God as well. God is saying, 'Even though it is hard, know that I will never leave you.'"

From then on, Kalpona could easily tell us what God was saying to her as she listened to his voice in her difficult memories.

Working With People Who Are Not Christian

So far, all of the examples I have shared in this section have been with Christians. What happens when you follow the same procedure with someone who is not a Christian?

Example: My life's deepest tragedy

I was sitting in a room with four South Asian women, three of whom were Muslim, and was preparing to lead a session on inner healing. The previous day, I had been invited to their workplace to lead a session on listening to God. Their experiences were so significant that they asked me to come again the next day. As I prepared for the second day, I decided I wanted to give them a life skill: learning how to process personal pain.

Listening to God with Muslims is a bit tricky. They typically see God as far off and not one with whom we can have a personal relationship. They see God as unembodied, without form. They see Jesus as a great prophet, but nothing more.

After explaining the inner healing process, I said a brief prayer and invited the four women to relax. I then invited them to see themselves in a pleasant place in their mind's eye. After a few minutes, I told them to think of a minor difficult event, perhaps a recent argument with a spouse or parent or something of that nature. I told them not to choose their life's deepest tragedy. I was a guest in this situation, and I did not want them to open deep wounds in an environment where there might not be an opportunity for resolution. After re-entering the difficult event, I invited them to see God or Jesus (whatever they felt comfortable with) coming to them as a person. I asked them to listen to what he said to them in their hearts. Then I waited.

After they opened their eyes, I gave these women an opportunity to share what had happened in their hearts. This had to be done carefully and without pressure. Sometimes deep personal issues should not be shared with colleagues or with me, a man.

Marifa began to speak. "Our brother told us not to choose our life's deepest sorrow.[5] But that is what I did. My deepest tragedy was when my father died six years ago. My life turned totally upside down." Marifa went on, "But perhaps it was better this way."

Five minutes ago, she had chosen the death of her father as her life's deepest tragedy. Now she was saying that it was better this way. I have no idea what Jesus spoke to the heart of this young Muslim woman, and it certainly did not seem appropriate to press for details, but Jesus's words brought a significant measure of healing. I hope this experience will be one of many steps that leads her to receiving Jesus as her Savior.

Matters to Keep in Mind

The process of inner healing is easy. This is not surprising because the Lord wants us to move into wholeness in all areas of our lives. We can do inner healing prayer alone with our journals, or we can do it with the help of others. We start by being with Jesus in a pleasant memory. After we can sense his presence and hear his voice, we walk with Jesus into a difficult memory. There, we listen for Jesus's words, which bring healing. Finally, we record the answers in a journal or share them verbally with the person helping us.

Although the process of inner healing prayer is easy, we should keep several matters in mind.

---

5. "Brother" is used as a term of respect for men in this culture. It is impolite to address a person of similar age or older by their given name unless the relationship is very close.

Prior relationships

Unless you are a professional counselor, it is wise to limit your inner healing prayers to people whom you know well. Apart from just a few exceptions (like the one mentioned above), most of the inner healing prayer sessions I have led have come up in the context of a discipling relationship. Inner healing prayer is a powerful tool in the discipleship process because we frequently encounter wounds and painful experiences in the life of the person we are discipling. At other times, inner healing prayers are the natural result of a conversation at the dinner table with close friends. I would be cautious about entering into inner healing prayer with someone I do not know.

Start with the easy issues, stay with the issues God leads us to

Start with easy matters as you begin to practice inner healing. Even in a very close discipling relationship, we may encounter situations that we are just not equipped to deal with yet. Some people have experienced extremely traumatic events, and we should be cautious about getting in over our heads. We should also be cautious about going beyond the capacity of the relationship we are in. In other words, we should not pry into the dark secrets of a person's life. If there is an issue and if the Lord believes it is important to bring up at this point in time, he will do so. The Lord's timing is much better than our own. A person may have an issue but may not be ready to deal with it. If the person does not want to go there, leave it until the person is ready.

Knowing when not to engage

I was traveling to a conference with an organizational leader and his wife, whom I'll call Sally. Sally was clearly a tremendously gifted woman. I enjoyed hearing her talk and jotted down some great ideas as I listened to her. Sally obviously had a close walk with the Lord and enjoyed spending time with him. But something else came through as we visited. Sally felt pain over not being valued as a woman in a Christian organization. That evening in my devotions, knowing I would be spending more time with Sally in the coming days, I thought of how easily the Lord could minister to the wounds she had sustained. Then I heard the Lord tell me clearly that I was not to engage with her on this subject. We are not called to help everyone, and it is important to hear when the Lord is telling us not to move ahead.

Sometimes the Lord says yes

Sammy was feeling a lot of work-related stress, so he set up a time when he could come to me for a coaching session. To my surprise, he brought his wife, Shetuli, with him. Shortly after our first session together, Shetuli contacted me privately and revealed a life of deep sexual brokenness. Immediately, my warning signals went up. I shouldn't touch this with a ten-foot pole. These cases are reserved for professional counselors who are trained in marriage and family therapy, not for a person like me with no formal qualifications in this area.

As I prayed about this, the Lord seemed to be telling me to go ahead. Still not sure, I checked with my mentors. Both encouraged me to move forward. That led to beginning an inner healing process with Shetuli and Sammy. Today, one year later, as I look over my notes from those sessions, I am astounded at what God did. In just three sessions, Shetuli went from being full of fears and practically unable to even close her eyes in prayer to being able to listen to Jesus easily.

Not everyone may need inner healing prayer

I have seen the power of inner healing prayer and watched very significant transformation occur after just a few sessions. On the other hand, I have also heard testimonies of people who were instantly healed from multi-year emotional trauma. Sometimes we find a great tool and assume it is for everyone. Let's not limit what God can do just to one technique or assume that everyone needs to go through the same process.

Solving All Your Problems?

Inner healing is very effective, but it cannot solve all a person's problems. The inner healing process presented in this chapter does not address cases where deliverance is needed. It does not address cases where growth in maturity is needed. James Wilder, in *Living From The Heart Jesus Gave You*, talks about "adult infants." These people have grown up physically but have not completed some of the tasks necessary for emotional maturity and therefore cannot take care of themselves emotionally.[6] While inner healing can dramatically remove blocks to spiritual growth and emotional health, it is not a substitute for practices that lead to maturity. We must not minimize the importance of faithfully following the Lord, being careful about what we allow our minds to dwell on (2 Cor 10:5), daily spiritual practices, fellowship with a solid body of believers, exercising faith, and personal discipline.

We have started to talk about how those who do not follow Jesus can hear his voice. We will cover this more in the next chapter.

6. Friesen et al., *The Heart Jesus Gave You*, 36.

Chapter 9

Listening in Outreach

The Christmas Party

OUR MUSLIM GUESTS WERE squished together on chairs, trunks, and stools around our living room. The snacks, games, and chitchat were over, and now they were listening to me tell them something about the meaning of Christmas. This year, for some reason, I had settled on the story of the prodigal son as my Christmas message. As I told the story, I understood why Jesus told stories. Our guests listened with rapt attention. When the story was over, I realized something else. The story of the prodigal son is quite shocking when you hear it for the first time. I told the story a second time and then asked the group what they thought the meaning was. Coming from their honor/shame worldview, several thought the father was shaming the errant son into being good. After further discussion, they worked out that the forgiving father in the story represented God and the son represents us in our tendency to wander away from him.

I then told them that all of us have become separated from God. Like the father in this story, God is waiting for us to return to him. Then I said, "I have a simple way of returning to God." I told them that if they were willing to participate, I could lead them in a meditative prayer through which they could return to God. For these educated, upper-class Muslims, the idea of a meditative prayer was not that unusual. After all, a number of meditation groups in society are trying to merge New Age teachings with traditional Islam.[1]

I told the story again. This time, I asked them to see a person walking on a village path. I asked them to see the surroundings and feel the heat and dust of the journey. As this person walked, he wondered how his father would receive him after all the things he had done. He rehearsed the speech he would make. Then I changed the story. I told my guests to see themselves on that path. I told them to think about the heat of the journey and the fear about what kind of reception they would receive. I had them thinking about what they would say to their father as they walked. Then I changed it again. I told them to see God himself in the form of a man running to meet them. He grabs them in an embrace. He holds them and tells them how glad he is that they have come home. When the story was over, a holy hush filled the room. I believe God was speaking to the hearts of those present.[2]

Can People from Other Religions Hear God's Voice?

"God doesn't hear the prayers of sinners," my friend was saying, "the only prayer from non-Christians that God will hear is a prayer of repentance." This was the argument among my Christian high school friends, but I can see now that this argument does not have biblical support. We see several cases in the Bible where God both heard and answered the prayers of people who did not yet know him. "One day at about three in the afternoon [Cornelius] had a vision. He distinctly saw an angel of God, who came to him and said, 'Cornelius!' Cornelius stared at him in fear. 'What is it, Lord?' he asked. The angel answered, 'Your prayers and gifts to the poor have come up as a memorial offering before God'" (Acts 10:3–4).

Not only does God hear the prayers of people who are not yet Christians, God speaks to them even when they are not seeking to hear his voice. God spoke to Nebuchadnezzar, both through a dream (Dan 4:4–27) and through a voice from heaven:

---

1. Meditation is a biblical concept (Gen 24:63; Josh 1:8; Ps 1:2; 119:15) but very different from the various forms of meditation practiced in South Asia. Islamic meditation, called Dhikr, involves repeating a short phrase until one enters a trancelike state. See https://en.wikipedia.org/wiki/Dhikr.

2. I realize that this was not a full and complete gospel presentation. But if we look at the life of Jesus, we don't usually see him giving a full gospel presentation either. He spoke in parables and gave as much information as his audience was willing to hear.

Twelve months later, as the king was walking on the roof of the royal palace of Babylon, he said, "Is not this the great Babylon I have built as the royal residence, by my mighty power and for the glory of my majesty?" Even as the words were on his lips, a voice came from heaven, "This is what is decreed for you, King Nebuchadnezzar: Your royal authority has been taken from you. You will be driven away from people and will live with the wild animals; you will eat grass like the ox. Seven times will pass by for you until you acknowledge that the Most High is sovereign over all kingdoms on earth and gives them to anyone he wishes." (Dan 4:29–32)

Fortunately, Nebuchadnezzar did acknowledge the Most High, and he was restored to his position. His successor was not so fortunate:

King Belshazzar gave a great banquet for a thousand of his nobles and drank wine with them . . . . As they drank the wine, they praised the gods of gold and silver, of bronze, iron, wood and stone. Suddenly the fingers of a human hand appeared and wrote on the plaster of the wall, near the lampstand in the royal palace. The king watched the hand as it wrote. His face turned pale and he was so frightened that his legs became weak and his knees were knocking. (Dan 5:1, 4–6)

God was speaking to King Belshazzar through a miraculous sign. I am certain God would have shown mercy to him if he would have responded immediately in deep repentance. But he did not so respond and was killed that night.

We see many other examples. God spoke to Pharaoh through dreams (Gen 41). God spoke to Abimelech about Abraham's wife (Gen 20:3–8). God spoke to the Philistines through signs when their idol fell before the ark of God (1 Sam 5:1–7). God speaking to non-believers is not merely an Old Testament phenomenon. Saul is one dramatic New Testament example:

Meanwhile, Saul was still breathing out murderous threats against the Lord's disciples. He went to the high priest and asked him for letters to the synagogues in Damascus, so that if he found any there who belonged to the Way, whether men or women, he might take them as prisoners to Jerusalem. As he neared Damascus on his journey, suddenly a light from heaven flashed around him. He fell to the ground and heard a voice say to him, "Saul, Saul, why do you persecute me?" "Who are you, Lord?" Saul asked. "I am Jesus, whom you are persecuting," he replied. "Now get up and go into the city, and you will be told what you must do." (Acts 9:1–6)

God desires to communicate with people who do not know him. If these few examples are any indication, he communicates with them frequently. Most of the time, however, the non-believer needs a Christian to help make sense of what God is saying, just like Ananias did for Saul (Acts 9:17–19). God doesn't need people to share the good news of salvation through Jesus. He can communicate on his own. However, instead of communicating his message directly, God has chosen to use us. A person rarely chooses to follow Jesus without the assistance of another disciple of Jesus.

Sitting Under the Gazebo

Ingrid and I were enjoying our holiday at the guest house of a mission hospital in the north of the country where we lived. The days were hot and humid, but in the evenings, the temperature cooled, and Ingrid and I enjoyed sitting under the gazebo, reading our books and spending time together. One evening, I was looking forward to some uninterrupted reading, but two other guests who were in the guest house that day came over to chat. Kalam and his colleague had been visiting the hospital as part of the non-government organization (NGO) work they were involved in.

I must have sufficiently concealed my irritation over the disruption of my idyllic reading time because Kalam didn't leave. I asked him about his hobbies and then told him that one of mine was listening to God. His attention piqued; I explained a little bit more. I told him that most Muslims see God as distant, but God loves us deeply and wants to communicate with us, just like a father wants to talk to his children.[3] I asked if he wanted to try it. When he answered in the affirmative, I led him in a listening session.

I told him to quiet his heart and to picture himself in a quiet, peaceful place. I asked him to imagine that God was coming to him in the form of a person. When he had an awareness of God's presence, I told him to ask, "God, how much do you love me?" He didn't share what he experienced, but his body language indicated that the time was significant for him. We exchanged phone numbers, and he promised to call me.

---

3. In many South Asian countries, you can tell a person's religion by hearing their name. Kalam is a Muslim name. The examples in this chapter are all of Muslims hearing God's voice.

Talking to a Businessman

Nasir was trying to start a handicraft business and was looking for advice. Sitting in my office, he talked about his business idea and showed me some pictures of his product samples. I listened to what he had to say but told him I had very little business experience. I said that he really needed God's advice. I explained that God speaks to people, but most of the time, we don't understand or even try to listen to what God is saying. I showed him where the Bible says, "Why do you complain to him that he responds to no one's words? For God does speak—now one way, now another—though no one perceives it" (Job 33:13–14).

I told him that God presents himself as knocking at the door of our hearts, desiring to come in and converse with us. Again, I opened my Bible and read, "Here I am! I stand at the door and knock. If anyone hears my voice and opens the door, I will come in and eat with that person, and they with me" (Rev 3:20).

Then I led him in a listening session and closed in a prayer. Afterward, he said that he felt happy, and he looked happy too.

Advice for Your Marriage

Sporsho and Brishti's marriage was falling apart. They lived in the same apartment building as us, two floors up, and their children were often in our home where "Auntie Ingrid" played with them or gave them crafts to do. Finally, Sporsho moved out, leaving Brishti with responsibility for two children, apartment rent, school fees, and no source of income. We had spent most of our time with Brishti, praying with her and listening to God together. Eventually (and miraculously, from our perspective), things settled down after a few weeks. Sporsho rented another flat in a different part of town, the family moved back in with him, and open hostility simmered down to cold war.

One day, while visiting them in their new home, I plucked up the courage to talk with Sporsho. As we walked around the exercise path near their home, Sporsho began to unburden his heart and fill in some of the gaps in the story that Brishti had conveniently left out. After talking for a while, I suggested that we sit down and listen to what God might have to say to him. We sat on a bench beside the exercise path and quieted our hearts. Sporsho felt God telling him that he needed to make sacrifices for the sake of his marriage.

Have You Seen the Man in White?

One evening, I was busy reading email on my phone and, as usual, not interested in being interrupted. But I had learned that interruptions are times that God will work if given the chance. Rakib, the friendly manager of the resort we were holidaying at, came over to chat. Our conversation ranged from Lalon Shah, a popular South Asian singer and philosopher; to God; and then to the teachings of Eckhart Tolle, a New Age spiritual teacher and best-selling author.

Knowing that I would soon be way out of my depth if we got into a philosophical discussion, I suggested we do a meditation and try to listen to God's voice. Rakib was immediately interested in this idea. I explained the process: God loves us and wants to talk to us; when he talks, he speaks in our heart. We usually perceive God's voice as thoughts. I then told him to close his eyes if he liked, take a few deep breaths, and go back in his mind to a peaceful place, perhaps a place he enjoyed in childhood. When he was settled in that memory, I asked him to look around and see God coming to him in the form of a person. When he was aware of someone with him, which he indicated by nodding his head, I told Rakib to ask God how he should seek him. I told him to open his eyes when he was finished.

As I waited, I prayed in my heart that Jesus would reveal himself to Rakib. Rakib clearly had a deeply meaningful spiritual experience, but it was unlike anything I expected. He saw himself at a pond in a tea plantation where he and his friends used to swim and play as children. He saw his mother there—his mother who had passed away ten years ago. She was happy and was trying to show him something, but he could not understand what she was saying or trying to show him.

If I thought I would be out of my depth in a philosophical discussion, I was way out of my depth now. This vision of his mother was both very significant to him and somewhat scary. I wondered if in some way she herself had heard the gospel and if in this vision she was trying to show him the Bible. On the other hand, initiating conversations with dead people seems to be forbidden in the Bible.

At this point, I didn't know where to take the conversation. I suspected God was in it, but I wasn't sure how, and I didn't want to fill his vision with artificial meaning created by me. So I changed the subject. Knowing of the many reports of Muslims seeing dreams of a man in white, a man whom they later identify as Jesus, I decided to ask Rakib about this.

His answer greatly surprised me. "Yes, I have seen him. Many times." Rakib went on, "I saw him in the clouds with his arms held out." Once Rakib had even drawn a picture of what he had seen and showed it to his brothers. They were impressed with the drawing, but Rakib never told them what inspired it. I told Rakib that many have seen a vision of a man in white, and they often later learn the man in white is Jesus. I then picked up my phone again and read from Acts 1 about Jesus ascending into heaven and being covered by clouds. He was interested to learn more, so I helped him download the Bible on his phone.

That conversation started Rakib on a spiritual search. Since then, he has read the gospels, watched the *Jesus* film, and has started reading the Old Testament. The following night, we met with his wife and had a time of prayer and listening to God with her as well. She said we were the most special visitors they had ever had at their resort.

From Listening to the Bible

Murshid, a friend with whom I had not had any contact for several years, happened to be in town again, and so he phoned me. I did the culturally appropriate thing and immediately invited him for lunch. When he arrived, he filled me in on his recent tragic history, mentioning both the death of his wife, whom he deeply loved, and the death of his father.

After listening to his story, I prayed for him. Afterward, he sat in silence for some time. When that happens, it is usually an indication that the Holy Spirit is working in the heart of the person. Since there seemed to be an open door to go further, I read some passages from the book of Job and explained a little about listening to God. Then I led him in a listening time. After telling Murshid to picture himself in a pleasant place, I asked him to look for the person whom God had sent to him. Instead of seeing a person come to him, he simply had an awareness of God's presence, which came easily to him. He then voiced a question in his heart to God and immediately received the answer, "Have patience. Things will be made right in time."

Murshid was surprised to receive an answer so quickly and wondered if that was an indication that he was simply hearing his own thoughts, not

God's voice. I opened the Bible to the book of James and read: "Brothers and sisters, as an example of patience in the face of suffering, take the prophets who spoke in the name of the Lord. As you know, we count as blessed those who have persevered. You have heard of Job's perseverance and have seen what the Lord finally brought about. The Lord is full of compassion and mercy" (James 5:10–11).

When he saw that the words he received matched very closely with what was written in Scripture, he was really encouraged. He concluded that this book (the Bible) was important and he should get one.

What Can We Learn from These Various Experiences?

After leading several Muslims and agnostics in listening experiences, I have come to the following conclusions.

God speaks to non-Christians

Listening with non-believers really works. God speaks to them, and sometimes the experience is powerful. God wants to talk to the people he has created, but they often need someone to introduce them to the idea of listening to God and help them interpret the experience. This is consistent with what we see in the Bible when we see that God interacts directly with people who do not know him. Both Paul (Acts 9) and Cornelius (Acts 10) needed interactions with people who already knew Jesus before they could move on in their walk with God.

Different beings may speak

One night, Ingrid and I were sitting outside with Nasiba, the wife of Rakib, mentioned above. I gave Nasiba a very brief gospel presentation and then asked her if she wanted to try listening to God. She was very eager to try this. I told Nasiba to see herself in a beautiful place. This time, instead of telling her to see God coming to her in human form, I asked her to look for the person sent from God. She reported that she had a sense of a person sitting next to her on her right side where it would make sense for a person to sit in our little circle. We sat in silence again for another listening time. I was praying in my heart that God would send some strong angels and protect her from any occult influence that might be present in her life. By then, Nasiba almost seemed to have gone into a trance. After waiting for several minutes, I finally interrupted her to ask what she was experiencing. She told us that she felt very good and very peaceful.

I had been trying to be more sensitive to the Holy Spirit myself in leading others in listening sessions, which required me to take some risks. Just then a risky question popped into my mind. "Tell her to ask the name of the person whom you saw with you." We quieted our hearts and listened again. Ingrid was listening too and asking the same question. She so wanted the answer to be "Jesus," but instead she heard "Gabriel" in her heart. Nasiba was too shy or uncertain to give an answer. After a bit of encouragement, she admitted that the name she heard in her heart was "Jibrail," the Arabic equivalent of Gabriel.

Although we normally expect God or Jesus to be the one communicating with us, we see many biblical examples of angels bringing messages from God. Examples include Joseph (Matt 1:20), Cornelius (Acts 10:3), Peter (Acts 12:7), and Paul (Acts 27:23).

Listening to God is an easy way to start spiritual conversations

After growing up in the church, I have heard many sermons on the need to share the gospel with non-Christians. Despite the well-intentioned preachers, I was left feeling guilty for not witnessing enough. This guilt led to pressure that led to performance anxiety, which was a terrible foundation on which to try to share my faith. Such guilt-driven conversations were rarely helpful and frequently degenerated into arguments about which religion is correct.

Talking about listening to God, on the other hand, is a different matter. It is interesting and engaging. Once you bring up the subject, people want to hear more. And it is relatively easy to bring up the subject. When I am in conversation with someone and sense that this might be the right place to talk about spiritual matters, I often bring up the topic of listening to God. At other times, I bring up the subject when the person I am talking with is worried about something or needs advice. In my experience, this kind of conversation works best when it is done on the foundation of a healthy, friendly relationship. I would not feel comfortable trying to help someone listen to God if our previous relationship was characterized by religious arguments. Learning to listen to God requires an environment of safety and trust.

It is best to use a simple procedure

I often start by reading Job 33:14. "For God does speak—now one way, now another—though no one perceives it." Although this verse is part of Elihu's speech, he is sharing a spiritual truth. God speaks—he speaks more than once, but people do not listen or understand what he is saying. The problem is not that God doesn't talk; the problem is that people do not listen or do not know how to listen.

After reading from Job, I go on to read 1 Thess 5:23. "May your whole spirit, soul and body be kept blameless at the coming of our Lord Jesus Christ." I point out that we, as humans, are composed of three parts: body, soul, and spirit. Since God is spirit, he will speak to our spirit or to our spiritual ears, not to our body or physical ears. We understand what is going on in our spirit as thoughts in our minds.

Then I have the person quiet his heart. The simplest way to do this is to tell the person to imagine himself in a very peaceful environment. Then I coach him to see God or a messenger from God coming to him in the form of a person to talk to him. Then I tell the person to ask a question and note the thoughts he receives in response. After the listening time is over, I ask the participant to share what he has experienced.

Some experience is necessary

I would not encourage anyone to try helping a non-Christian to hear God's voice until he himself has had quite a bit of practice helping Christians to hear God's voice. Working with non-Christians adds extra complexity to the experience. It takes practice to figure out what to say to begin the experience so that the person of the religion that you are interacting with can relate. With Christians, I almost always invite the listener to interact with Jesus. With Muslims, I have found that this does not work as well because they see Jesus primarily as a prophet. Instead, with Muslims, I invite them to picture God coming to them in the form of a man, or I invite them to look for the person or messenger sent from God. In both Hebrew and

Greek, the root meaning of "angel" is messenger.[4] My overall approach is to seek to introduce the person I am sitting with to God through hearing his voice. At this stage, I am not concerned about right theology and the finer points of religion. That is for later, maybe even years later, if that is how long it takes for the person to truly know God through Jesus.

On occasion, a listening experience will not be helpful. If the person you are talking with has a history of occult influence, I would discourage leading him in a listening experience; otherwise, the results might be very confusing. If the person is very unsettled or struggles with a lot of fears, then it might be more appropriate to pray for deliverance from fear than to lead them in a listening experience.

A listening experience is only the beginning

Listening experiences are one step in the process of coming to know Jesus. Participating in a listening experience awakens a person to spiritual matters and invites them to explore further. For example, Farhad accepted an invitation to come to church after a listening experience. Frequently, the listening experience provides an opportunity to read from the Bible to substantiate what just happened. Murshid, whom I previously mentioned, downloaded the Bible on his phone after a listening experience.

Although she had several very significant listening experiences, Brishti never got to the place of regularly reading Scripture on her own. When her crisis was over, her desire to interact on a spiritual level seemed to vanish as well. Attempting to listen to God without engagement with Scripture and ongoing spiritual contact with a follower of Jesus does not seem to lead someone to a salvation experience.

There Are No Magic Bullets

Sometimes we encounter a particular method of engaging with people spiritually and assume this is the magic bullet; this is the best way to interact with non-believers. Leading a person in a listening experience is one way to engage with someone on a spiritual level. But this is not the only way to lead people to Jesus. Some people begin their spiritual search on an intellectual level. Some come to faith primarily through a study of the Word.

4. *Mickelson's*, s. v. "H4397 mal'ak" and "G32 aggelos."

For others, experiencing a healing or an answer to prayer is a key factor. Listening to God is just one tool in our spiritual toolbox. Let's use whatever tools we have available to us.

Conclusion

Why This Probably Won't Work for You

My Journey

UNFORTUNATELY, EVERYTHING I HAVE written in this book probably won't work for you. It didn't work for me either until I discovered one important ingredient.

When I was in high school, I read a book about a pastor who learned how to listen to Jesus. He started his journey by opening his Bible at random and asking God to speak to him. God did speak to him that way, and then God led him to other ways of hearing his voice. God warned him about what was coming. God led him to change his plans at times. God answered his prayers in amazing ways. I thought it would be great to have a relationship with God like that, but I had no one to guide me in the process.

After high school, I attended Bible college for a year. There, I read *Hearing Heart* and *Wayfarer in the Land* by Hannah Hurnard. In these books, Hurnard relates how she was transformed from a shy, stammering girl to a missionary in Palestine. She developed an acute ability to hear God's voice in the form of thoughts in her heart. I longed to have the same kind of relationship with God. I tried to listen to God's voice speaking into my thoughts, but I quickly became confused. I had no one to help me work through my confusion and mistakes, and so I eventually gave up on the process.

After Bible college, I went to a large university to study engineering. On campus, I found a little Bible study group made up of people who zealously encouraged their members to spend lots of time in prayer. They frequently talked about how God spoke to them. They encouraged their members to cry out to God and ask him to speak, but they never explained *how* God speaks. For them, God's voice usually seemed to come after they had spent lots of time in prayer in deep emotional angst. Then they would open their Bible at random, and their eyes would light upon a verse that addressed their situation.[1] I tried this too, and at times, God did indeed speak to me. But this was not a very reliable method of hearing God's voice, and so I gave up on that method too. It would have been helpful if someone could have succinctly explained to me how God speaks.

After university and a stint in the workplace, I sensed God's call into missions through a conference at Urbana.[2] If I wasn't too embarrassed to share it, I would tell you about the time I tried to use lots to determine which country God would have me serve in. Short version: I ended up with more confusion than clarity.

At every stage, I longed to experience God's voice, and I did experience God's voice from time to time, but it was not a reliable form of communication for me. I once attended a retreat put on by the zealous university group. I had heard all those testimonies about God speaking to people, and I longed for the same thing too. I went out to the forested area on the retreat campground, took off my shoes, knelt in the grass, and prayed and wept, asking God to speak to me. I don't know what I was expecting, but I did hear God's voice that time. With a clarity equal to someone speaking in my ears, I heard God's voice in my thoughts. "I love you, Neil." I wiped my eyes and put on my shoes. Even though it was not what I was expecting, I couldn't honestly deny that God had spoken to me. But hearing God's voice did not become a regular and reliable experience in my life.

---

1. Although the practice of opening the Bible at random and asking God to speak is roundly condemned from the pulpit, many people have done this at some point in their lives. Jack Deere, a former Dallas Seminary professor, relates how, after a woman was freed from demonic oppression in his church through the ministry of a visiting speaker, he was afraid of the ridicule he would face when the word of what happened got out. "So I did something I would have mocked a year earlier. In the dark, I asked God to speak to me, opened my Bible, and let my finger fall randomly on the page. It landed on Luke's story of the Gerasene demoniac, the man whom Jesus had freed of thousands of demons . . . . God had come to our church in power to free a woman from demonic oppression, and I woke up ready to ask God not to come back in that way. But not anymore." Deere, *Even in our Darkness*, 163.

2. See https://urbana.org/ for information on the Urbana Student Missions Conference.

A number of years later, I ran across Karl Lehman's book, *The Immanuel Approach*, on inner healing and through this became convinced that not only does God speak to us in our pain, he will speak to us frequently if we let him. Then I started reading *Spent Matches* by Roy Moran, a book on discipleship. Through that book, I concluded that a key component of discipleship was learning how to hear God's voice. I thought I should try discipling someone by teaching that person how to hear God's voice. The only problem with my project was that I wasn't very good at hearing God's voice myself.

Then I met Clinton at a conference. He was simply an interesting stranger with whom I fell into conversation. We agreed to meet by Skype some weeks later. It turned out that Clinton knew a lot about hearing God's voice and was great at it. Clinton led me into a relationship with God where hearing God's voice became a regular occurrence in my life. When I ran into the inevitable difficulties and periods of confusion, Clinton walked me through them. I soon concluded that it is a lot easier to learn how to listen to God's voice if you have a mentor, coach, or discipler to help you through the inevitable difficult parts in the journey. Clinton became my mentor. I would have given up if he had not been present to coach me through the confusing times.

Listening to God is easy. This is not surprising because God wants to talk to us. But we will face problems along the way, and when we struggle and become confused, we need someone to help us. Jesus demonstrated the best strategy when he first made twelve disciples and then told them to go and make disciples of others. If you are just starting your journey of listening to Jesus, please find a mentor or discipler who can help you when you get stuck.

Mentoring Others

Some South Asian countries are notorious for corruption in the medical sector. Doctors routinely prescribe tests and operations that patients don't need because they receive a percentage of the fee for the procedure that the patient pays. I had been mentoring Fayez for several months, and one of the first subjects we covered was how to listen to Jesus. Then one day, Fayez experienced acute pain in the abdomen. He went to a doctor to get checked out and was soon admitted to a local hospital. The doctor told him he needed an emergency appendicitis operation. Fayez was facing a potentially very large hospital fee for an operation he might not need. That night, alone in his hospital room, he decided to ask Jesus about this. He had a vision of Jesus waving dismissively, indicating that this sickness was nothing to be concerned about. The next morning, Fayez phoned his wife and told her that he was coming home. He soon completely recovered and, shortly after, had a chance to be checked out by a trusted doctor in a mission hospital in another part of the country. The doctor assured him that there was no indication he had ever had appendicitis.

One of my great joys has been seeing other people learn how to listen to Jesus. It is a delight to watch as Jesus interacts lovingly with the person. Many times, my role is simply to introduce a person to Jesus, and the Lord takes it from there. As they listen to Jesus, their lives are changed. They move into greater emotional and spiritual health. Their desire to spend time with the Lord increases. They begin to bring transformation into their spheres of influence. It is an even greater joy when they step out with great faith and courage and teach others to hear God's voice.

Changing the World

I am convinced that if every Christian learned how to listen to the voice of Jesus and obeyed, the world would be changed. Christians would get over their emotional dysfunctions, families would experience harmony, churches would see their true purpose, the lost would be reached, and abusive structures in society would be transformed. Jesus would be the true head of his church, leading an army of disciples who know his will and do it. Will you be part of this army? Will you choose to listen to his voice daily?

Afterword

*The Church Owes the World
an Encounter With God*

NEIL'S STORY PARALLELS MY story. I began by being taught by the Western church that God no longer speaks. However, ultimately the passionate hunger of my heart to hear God's voice brought me to the revelation that indeed, his sheep DO hear his voice! Not only is hearing God's voice easy enough for children to do (actually it's easier than for adults), it is the most life-transforming skill one will ever acquire, and passing it on to others is one of the most rewarding experiences of life.

The life of Jesus and the writing of the Bible did not take place in the Western hemisphere. It took place in the Middle East. So to reduce the Bible and Christianity to the precepts of Western scholasticism is to do it an extreme disservice to say the very least!

Neil shared the following:

> If discipleship depends on my ability to create interesting content that keeps people engaged from meeting to meeting, then disciple-ship is hard. If discipleship depends on knowing how to solve the problems of my disciples, then discipleship is hard. If discipleship depends on my ability to motivate a person to behave a certain way and do certain activities, such as evangelism, daily prayer, and Bible study, then discipleship is hard. But if discipleship is showing people how they can live a life in conversation with Jesus, then discipleship is easy. I am no longer responsible to bring about change. I am no longer responsible to produce right behavior. That is Jesus's job. My job is merely to introduce the person to

a conversational relationship with Jesus and then check in from time to time to make sure the relationship is still active.

We realize with shock and excitement, *"I can live the Bible!"* Passion is ignited. Hearts are set on fire. Personal revival breaks out. The River of the Holy Spirit, which contains God's wisdom, power, an, emotions, flows freely within the heart of the believer. This River originates at the throne of God (Rev 22). We become aware that the flow within us is the River of the Holy Spirit (John 7:37–39).

All I need to do is to *believe* in this River and then tune to its flow. When my eyes are fixed on Jesus, flowing thoughts become his voice, flowing pictures his visions, and flowing emotions his emotions.

We can tune to his River and release Jesus to every person and into every situation we face. We can live as Jesus lived, out of our Father's initiative (John 5:19, 20, 30), as we unite faith and flow. With this revelation of the indwelling River of the Holy Spirit, the church can offer the world a living *encounter* with the living God.

This book is practical. Neil teaches you: 1) what God's voice sounds like, 2) how to quiet down to prepare yourself to hear God, 3) how to see a vision and interpret dreams, and 4) how to test the revelation you receive against Scripture (plus other means) to ensure that what you received has come from God. Neil honors the fact that we see through a glass darkly so not every vision and word we get will be 100 percent pure, but that doesn't deter us from pursuing a relationship with our divine lover.

In my daily conversations with Patti, my wife, my ability to understand her words and perspectives is not 100 percent accurate, but that doesn't mean I stop listening to her voice. I passionately desire a love relationship with Patti, so I dialogue with her, even though I am aware that her thought processes are very different from mine and I do not fully understand all the nuances of what she is saying. I enjoy a love relationship with Patti so much that this enjoyment far overshadows my need to perfectly comprehend the nuance of every word that comes from her lips. The same is true of my relationship with my divine lover.

Jesus is clear: "My sheep hear my voice" (John 10:27 KJV). These are his words. This is his guarantee. It's his integrity on the line. After ten years of not knowing how easy it was to hear his voice and appropriate this wonderful promise from Jesus, I stepped out with understanding and faith and began listening to and honoring his River which flows within me. Everything in my life changed.

One thing Jesus spoke to me in 1979 was a commission. He said we would *"saturate the world with communion with God."* Now, forty years later, millions recognize his voice easily in their everyday lives. On just our website alone we list more than fifty books, written by others, which are filled with examples of God speaking. Such books were almost completely unheard of forty years ago.

Jesus spoke again today as I am writing this:

> Mark, the revival has begun. My voice is sweeping the world. My presence is descending upon my church. My power is being made manifest. Now is the day of salvation. Now is the day of the harvest. Now is the best of times. Now is the day to plunder the enemy's ground. Lift your eyes for your redemption draws near. This is the time for expectations to be realized, for faith to be rewarded, for revelation to be fulfilled. Today is the day of the Lord. Watch and see the hand of the Lord. Behold, all will be amazed. Behold, all will be amazed. Behold, all will be amazed saith the Lord of Hosts. Watch and see the salvation of the Lord. It shall be a worldwide revival such as the world has never seen. It shall release my glory throughout the earth. Watch and see the salvation of the Lord.

My prayer is that you enter into this revival as you incorporate what you've read in this book and discover how easy it is to hear your lover's voice.

Mark Virkler
Founder, Communion with God Ministries
www.cwgministries.org/4keys
President, Christian Leadership University
Author of *4 Keys to Hearing God's Voice*

Appendix 1

Resources for Further Study

LISTENING TO GOD IS a huge subject. Each person who writes about these matters brings a unique perspective, revealing another facet of the way God speaks. No one person understands it all. Below, I list several books that have been helpful to me on my journey. The books are arranged roughly as they relate to the chapters in my book, enabling the reader to go deeper on subjects of interest. While each of these books has been helpful to me, I do not agree with all that is written in each one. My philosophy is to take what is good, right, and scriptural from each one and leave the rest. Or in biblical terms, as applied to prophecy, "Test everything. Hold on to the good" (1 Thess 5:21).

Chapter 1: Are We Missing Something?

For a defense of signs and wonders and of God speaking personally today, I recommend two books by Jack S. Deere. *Surprised by the Power of the Spirit* and *Surprised by the Voice of God* are well-researched works but note that Deere's goal in these books is not to give a how-to method of hearing God's voice. For readers interested in a deep theological justification for hearing God's voice, Dallas Willard's *Hearing God* is for you. The mere mortals among us may prefer an easier book to read.

For those who would rather learn by looking at the life of another person, the following autobiographies may appeal to you. Hannah Hurnard's *Hearing Heart* and *Wayfarer in the Land* is a delightful two-part autobiography describing how the author learned to hear God's voice. The story takes the reader from her stammering childhood to a fruitful missionary career.

Mary Geegh, a missionary to India, wrote about her experiences in 1900. *God Guides* is a compilation of accounts of her listening experiences. Once you start it, you will find it hard to put down.

Joyce Huggett in *Listening to God* takes the reader on her journey into contemplative prayer and then into the charismatic expression of Christianity. She describes the various ways God spoke to her in different seasons of her life. Although there is much to learn here, she never gives a simple how-to method of listening to Jesus.

Chapter 2: A Simple Method of Listening to Jesus

God is not limited to any one particular way of speaking, and he certainly needs no methods. It is we who need the methods. When we are learning a new task, a step-by-step method is helpful. The following resources give simple methods anyone can follow. I found Brad Jersak's *Can You Hear Me? Tuning in to the God Who Speaks* easy to read and very practical. It also provides many simple listening exercises for the reader.

But what if you want just one chapter and not a full book? I discovered Rusty Rustenbach's *Listening and Inner-Healing Prayer* after I had written my own manuscript and was surprised at the similarity to mine in the chapter on how to listen to God. See "Chapter 4: Principles of Listening Prayer" for a great one-chapter explanation of how to hear God's voice.

If you would rather listen than read, Mark Virkler's teaching on hearing God's voice is easy to find online. Virkler is a humorous and engaging speaker. You can sign up to receive his free three-part video teaching series here www.cwgMinistries.org/4keys. You can also read Mark and Patti Virkler's *4 Keys To Hearing God's Voice*.

Chapter 3: Does God Speak Through Dreams?

There are many books on dream interpretation. Unfortunately, many of them are dream symbol dictionaries. While symbol dictionaries can sometimes help, consulting a symbol dictionary is often not the best way to understand a dream since symbols are unique to the dreamer. Herman Riffel's

Dream Interpretation: A Biblical Understanding goes much deeper and is by far the best book on the subject I have come across.

For those who want a quick overview of biblical dream interpretation, I recommend the following paper by Mark and Patti Virkler: "Principles of Christian Dream Interpretation," available for download at https://revdonc. files.wordpress.com/2010/01/christian-dream-interpretation.pdf.

Chapter 4: Seeing Visions

Blake Healy was apparently born with the ability to see into the spiritual realm. His book, *The Veil: An Invitation to the Unseen Realm*, is a very interesting story that ends with some practical tips on learning to see spiritual things. Michael Van Vlymen believes that all of us can have our spiritual eyes opened. In *How to See in the Spirit: A Practical Guide on Engaging the Spirit Realm* he encourages his readers to spend much time in prayer, asking God to open their spiritual eyes.

Chapter 5: Mistakes and Discernment

Several of the books mentioned in this section deal with mistakes. See "Chapter 13: Many Mistakes" in Joyce Huggett's *Listening to God* and "Chapter 4: Principles of Listening Prayer" in Rusty Rustenbach's *Listening and Inner-Healing Prayer*.

Chapter 6: Understanding the Spiritual Realm

Numerous authors and speakers give their understanding of the spiritual realm and of what it means to be human. The best five-minute teaching I have found on this subject was given by Pastor Ken Vance of Vertical Church, "The Difference Between The Spirit & The Soul" on YouTube https://youtu.be/HMj1iLr8FMw.

Chapter 7: Listening in Discipleship

Several of my ideas on discipleship were catalyzed by Roy Moran's *Spent Matches: Igniting the Signal Fire for the Spiritually Dissatisfied*. He shows how knowledge-based approaches to discipleship lack effectiveness. He talks about the importance of disciples making disciples. He emphasizes obedience as a core value in discipleship. He sees the Discovery Bible Study process as the means to put all these principles together. I loved the first part of this book. The second half focused on the Discovery Bible Study method. While this is a great system, it can turn into a mental exercise that does not always result in a person hearing from the Lord.

Chapter 8: Listening and Inner Healing

Karl Lehman's *The Immanuel Approach: For Emotional Healing and for Life* was a key factor that set me on the journey of learning how to hear God's voice in a practical way. His book is massive, at over 700 pages, but extraordinarily helpful for those who want to learn how to work through their inner pain with Jesus. For those who might not want to read the whole book, Lehman has a lot of excellent material on his website https://www.immanuelapproach.com/book/, including a draft version of his book.

For those who do a lot of inner healing ministry with others, I would recommend Charles Kraft's *Two Hours to Freedom*. One of my mentors joked that the book should be called *Two Hours to Freedom Ten Times*. Perhaps an expert counselor can work through a person's entire life, processing all the pain and dealing with any demonic oppression in just two hours. In my experience, it takes a lot more time. Nevertheless, Kraft gives a solid, systematic approach that has helped many people achieve freedom.

If you want a workbook style approach that you can use on your own, I recommend Rusty Rustenbach's *Listening and Inner-Healing Prayer: Meeting God in the Broken Places*. Readers can work through the exercises in this book alone at their own pace or with a prayer partner.

Appendix 2

Answering Common Objections

MANY HAVE QUESTIONS AND concerns about the idea of God speaking to people today. In this appendix, I briefly address five common objections.

The book of Hebrews teaches us that God does not continue to speak.

The opening verses to the book of Hebrews say: "In the past God spoke to our ancestors through the prophets at many times and in various ways, but in these last days he has spoken to us by his Son, whom he appointed heir of all things, and through whom also he made the universe" (Heb 1:1–2).

These verses highlight a contrast. In the past, God spoke through the prophets, but later, he spoke through Jesus's life, sacrificial death, and resurrection. Some therefore assume that since God has spoken through his Son, he does not continue to speak. The problem with this view is that it negates other accounts of God speaking to people after Christ's ascension. The Bible tells of many post-ascension accounts of God speaking to people through a vision (Acts 9:10–16; 10:9–19; 16:6–10), through a prophet (Acts 11:28; 21:10–11), through an angel (Acts 27:23), and through direct communication by the Holy Spirit (Acts 10:19; 13:2). The whole book of Revelation would have to be discounted if God's voice ended with Jesus's time on earth.

God's revelation through Jesus could be compared to an author's magnum opus. The completion of a magnum opus, however, does not mean the author will never speak another word.

God no longer speaks since we have the completed canon of Scripture.

Many have been taught that God no longer directly communicates with individuals about practical matters in their lives because the canon of Scripture is closed. Everything we need is in the Bible, and so we can no longer expect our heavenly Father to communicate specifically with us.

Many authors have dealt extensively with this large topic.[1] I will only comment briefly. One justification for this point of view is found here: "Love never fails. But where there are prophecies, they will cease; where there are tongues, they will be stilled; where there is knowledge, it will pass away. For we know in part and we prophesy in part, but when completeness comes, what is in part disappears" (1 Cor 13:8–10).

Prophecies about specific matters in a person's life are thought to be an example of the incomplete. Now we have the completed Scripture, so the incomplete forms of prophecy and other revelatory gifts described in 1 Cor 12:8–10 have disappeared.

This perspective is erroneous because Paul gives no inkling he was thinking of a completed scriptural canon in this passage. Instead, Paul is referring to the end of the age when we dwell with Jesus forever. At that future point in time, we will no longer need prophecy, speaking in tongues, or revealed knowledge because we will see Jesus face-to-face. Prior to that point in time, we can only "know in part" (1 Cor 13:12).

God only speaks through the Bible.

Many who admit that God does speak personally claim that God only speaks through the Bible. To examine this claim, let's look at how God interacted with people in the New Testament period. Those who lived at that time had Scripture. We refer to this Scripture as the Old Testament. Jesus demonstrated that the Old Testament was sufficient to explain what people needed to know about himself. "He said to them, 'How foolish you are, and how slow to believe all that the prophets have spoken! Did not the Messiah have to suffer these things and then enter his glory?' And beginning with Moses and all the Prophets, he explained to them what was said in all the Scriptures concerning himself" (Luke 24:25–27).

1. Deere, *Power of the Spirit*, 141–42.

Despite the existence and sufficiency of this Scripture, God frequently chose to speak to people outside of this Scripture. For example, Peter would have known such messianic passages as Isa 42:1–7 that speak of the Messiah as a light to the Gentiles. The Holy Spirit could have impressed such a passage of Scripture on Peter's heart and used that to prepare him to receive the emissaries of the Gentile Cornelius. What did Peter receive instead? A fantastic vision of a sheet containing animals being let down from heaven (Acts 10:10–13).

If God had intended that we would only hear his voice from passages of Scripture, then surely, we would expect to see some indication of this in the Bible. Instead, we see biblical passages teaching the church how to appropriately deal with God-given prophetic words that are not part of Scripture (1 Cor 14:6, 27–31; 1 Thess 5:19–21).

We don't need God to speak to us about practical life issues.

Some may claim that since we have the Bible, we have all we need for life and godliness; therefore, we don't need God to speak to us about specific circumstances in our lives. Such a claim is not supported by scriptural examples. In the book of Acts, we see many instances where God spoke to people specifically about their present life circumstances. God spoke through Agabus about a coming famine (Acts 11:28), allowing the Christians in Antioch to send help to the Christians in Judea. God specifically called Paul and Barnabas to missionary work (Acts 13:2). God guided Paul and his companions when they were confused on their missionary journey (Acts 16:6–10). God encouraged Paul and told him what the future would hold when he was on a ship in a storm (Acts 27:23–24).

If we admit God speaks and reveals things to us today, then we are adding to the pages of Scripture.

For Christians, the Bible is our authority, the standard by which we measure all subsequent revelation. When we claim that God continues to speak to us today, we are neither adding to Scripture nor claiming that what we receive has the same authority as the written Word of God. We freely admit we are imperfect and do not always hear God correctly. This is why the

Bible gives instructions about testing the words we receive from God (1 Thess 5:21). When the church at Corinth practiced receiving and speaking out prophetic words from God, Paul assumed that some might speak in error. Therefore he said, "And if a revelation comes to someone who is sitting down, the first speaker should stop" (1 Cor 14:30).

Appendix 3

Some Thoughts on Interpreting the Bible

THE PRESUPPOSITIONS WE BRING to the Bible and to the interpretative process can greatly limit our openness to God's voice in our lives. If we assume God no longer speaks to people personally, then, for the Christian, the Bible becomes a document from which we extract principles for life, using our powers of intellect combined with rules of interpretation. I will assume very few of my readers still hold this perspective.

If we believe God does speak personally but has limited himself to only speaking to us through the Bible, then the way we interpret the Bible will have a big impact on how we understand God's voice. If, holding an even broader perspective, we believe God speaks in a wide variety of ways, not just through the pages of Scripture, then we still need to interpret the Bible correctly in order to verify that we are hearing from God accurately.

In this appendix, I will look at one of the most common approaches to interpreting the Bible and point out a couple of weaknesses with this approach. Then I will show how this approach can be expanded to enable us to learn all God wants us to learn from Scripture.

A Typical Approach to Interpreting the Bible

Gordon Fee and Douglas Stuart in their book, *How to Read the Bible for All Its Worth*, present the following rules for Bible interpretation:

- A text cannot mean what it never could have meant to its author or his or her readers.

- Whenever we share comparable particulars (i.e., similar specific life situations) with the first-century setting, God's Word to us is the same as his Word to them.

- When the particulars are different, we need to find a clear principle that transcends the historical particularity to which it is applied. This principle may only be applied in genuinely comparable situations.[1]

Simplifying this process and turning it into a three-step approach, InterVarsity Christian Fellowship and other groups have popularized the Inductive Bible Study Method.[2] In this method, one is taught to *observe* what the text said to the original audience, then *interpret* what it means to us, and finally *apply* the text to our own lives. "Inductive Bible study is an approach to God's Word focusing on three basic steps that move from a focus on specific details to a more general, universal principle. Through these three steps, we apply inductive reasoning, which is defined as the attempt to use information about a specific situation to draw a conclusion. The steps are observation (what does it say?), interpretation (what does it mean?), and application (what does it mean for my life?)."[3]

This approach to biblical interpretation, which I refer to as the "universal principle approach," is a great method of Bible study, particularly for those with an intellectual bent. I have no doubt God has spoken to many people through this method of engaging with Scripture. The universal principle approach keeps us from going off on strange theological tangents. This approach prevents us from reading our own messages into the text. But the universal principle approach can limit our understanding of the Word if we are not careful. I see two weaknesses that can arise when the universal principle approach is viewed as the only valid way to approach Scripture.

---

1. Fee, Stuart, *How to Read the Bible*, 64–65. The authors show how these principles apply to the Epistles, and then, with some adjustments, apply the same principles to the whole Bible.

2. Olesberg, "How to Do Inductive Bible Study."

3. Got Questions Ministries, "What is Inductive Bible Study?"

Weaknesses of the Universal Principle Approach

The problem with abstraction

Finding a universal principle is dependent on the ability to think abstractly. For those who have been raised in an oral culture and for those with limited formal education, abstraction is difficult, if not impossible. David Epstein describes in fascinating detail the work of a psychologist studying pre-modern people in Russia in 1931.

> In every cognitive direction, the minds of pre-modern citizens were severely constrained by the concrete world before them. With cajoling, some solved the following logic sequence: "Cotton grows well where it is hot and dry. England is cold and damp. Can cotton grow there or not?" They had direct experience growing cotton, so some of them could answer (tentatively and when pushed) for a country they had never visited. The same exact puzzle with different details stumped them: "In the Far North, where there is snow, all bears are white. Novaya Zemlya is in the Far North and there is always snow there. What colors are the bears there?" That time, no amount of pushing could get the remote villagers to answer. They would respond only with principles. "Your words can be answered only by someone who was there," one man said, even though he had never been to England but had just answered the cotton question.[4]

If the only correct way to interpret Scripture depends on a high level of abstraction, we are in danger of preventing people who have not received a high level of Western-style education from applying Scripture to their lives. Former seminary professor Jack Deere pushes back on the idea that a high level of intelligence or education is required to understand the Bible. "Christian scholarship is not nearly as important as Christian scholars have led us to believe. The American church is easily deceived in this matter, for the Western world worships intelligence and education. As far as I know, neither the Bible in general, nor Christ and his apostles in particular, ever commend intelligence as having any significant role in understanding God or his Word."[5]

4. Epstein, *Range*, 46.
5. Deere, *Voice of God*, 258.

The problem of cultural conditioning

The other problem we face in using the universal principle approach to interpreting Scripture is that the principles we derive from our study of Scripture are strongly conditioned by our cultural upbringing.

In Matt 14:14–15, we see a need for provision. "When Jesus landed and saw a large crowd, he had compassion on them and healed their sick. As evening approached, the disciples came to him and said, 'This is a remote place, and it's already getting late. Send the crowds away, so they can go to the villages and buy themselves some food.'"

Further in the chapter, we see how Jesus took the little they had and multiplied it. Most Bible teachers will find a universal principle relating to the importance of giving the little we have to Jesus so that he can multiply it. That is very nice, but I am quite sure that is not what Jesus had in mind when he said to them, "They do not need to go away. You give them something to eat" (v. 16).

The disciples had already been sent out. They had already healed the sick and driven out demons (Matt 10). They would have been familiar with miracles of provision in the Old Testament, such as the widow's flour and oil (1 Kgs 17:9–16), the widow's oil (2 Kgs 4:1–7), and multiplied bread (2 Kgs 4:42–44). Now, Jesus was asking his disciples to step up to a higher level of faith and perform a miracle of provision themselves. We are not normally taught this in our churches on Sunday mornings because our cultural conditioning tells us that such things do not happen these days.

Luke 8:22–25 tells us how Jesus calmed a storm.

> One day Jesus said to his disciples, "Let us go over to the other side of the lake." So they got into a boat and set out. As they sailed, he fell asleep. A squall came down on the lake, so that the boat was being swamped, and they were in great danger. The disciples went and woke him, saying, "Master, Master, we're going to drown!" He got up and rebuked the wind and the raging waters; the storm subsided, and all was calm. "Where is your faith?" he asked his disciples. In fear and amazement they asked one another, "Who is this? He commands even the winds and the water, and they obey him."

I have not once heard a message in church where the primary principle derived from this passage is that the disciples should have calmed the storm themselves. But that is exactly what Jesus is saying to them when he asks, "Where is your faith?" The disciples would have known the stories from the Old Testament where God's people exerted authority over nature. Samuel called down thunder and rain during the time of wheat harvest (1 Sam 12:16–18). Both Elijah (2 Kgs 2:8) and Elisha (2 Kgs 2:13–14) divided the Jordan River by slapping it with a cloak. Moses divided the Red Sea by stretching his hand over it (Exod 14:15–22). Jesus expected his disciples to exert authority over nature, just as those in the Old Testament did.

Lest we too quickly jump to the conclusion that controlling nature is not within the purview of modern-day disciples of Jesus, we should remember that many examples of similar things have taken place in our day and age.[6]

Example: Don't delay me or I will get caught in the storm

It had been a scorchingly hot period in our region in the summer of 2008, and the crops urgently needed rain. During the house church meeting Rupa asked Fazil to pray for rain. Fazil protested that anyone could pray. Still, Rupa insisted that Fazil be the one to pray, reminding him of how the prophet Elijah had prayed for rain in the Bible. So Fazil prayed. When the meeting was over, Fazil was in a hurry to get on his motorcycle to drive to his home some fifty kilometers away. Another man who was present at the meeting wanted to chat and wondered what the big hurry was. Fazil responded, "If you delay me by even five minutes, I won't be able to get home before the rain comes." With a note of mockery, this man responded, "What, in this burning heat, you are going to be caught by rain?" Sure enough, heavy rain came, and Fazil had to take shelter under a tree about five minutes away from his home.[7]

A Biblical Approach to the Bible

From personal experience, I have found that those without a lot of formal education struggle with abstraction and are often unable to find a universal principle from a Scripture passage. On the other hand, those with lots of formal education and who can find abstract principles from a Bible passage

---

6. See, for example, Haye, *Tread Upon the Lion*. Tommie Titcombe was an early missionary of the now well-known mission, SIM.

7. Fazil personally told me this story in 2020, and I then verified it via phone call with Rupa. The only detail the two were not in agreement about was the exact year in which the event happened.

may be so influenced by their cultural conditioning that they cannot see the message in the text if it runs counter to their worldview.

Even Jesus and the New Testament writers did not usually look for a universal principle when they handled the Old Testament. Is there a way of looking at the Bible that does not close our eyes to the possibilities of what God can and wants to do in our own age? How ought we to interpret the Bible? First Cor 10:11 gives us a suggestion: "These things happened to them as examples and were written down as warnings for us, on whom the culmination of the ages has come."

Even illiterate people can look for an example to follow when they hear a passage of Scripture. I suppose God could have made the Bible so complicated that only those with years of formal study would understand it. Yet somehow, I think he intended for even children to understand the Bible. Children learn primarily by imitation.

Without negating the value of the universal principle method of interpreting Scripture, we can expand upon it by appreciating the value of examples. Everything in Scripture is in some way an example to us. The entire Old Testament sacrificial system is an example prefiguring Christ's final sacrifice. (See Heb 9–10.) Jesus intentionally performed many actions, such as washing his disciples' feet (John 13:15), as examples for his followers. In 1 Tim 1:16, Paul saw even his own conversion as an example illustrating the patience of Christ.

Paul said, "Follow my example, as I follow the example of Christ" (1 Cor 11:1). Does this example only have to do with his character and how he preached the gospel? Does it not also have to do with how he listened to God? As we seek to interpret and apply Scripture to our daily lives, we must consider that Scripture contains examples of how God interacted with people in the past. These interactions are examples to us, showing how God interacts with us today.

Acknowledgments

I WISH TO EXPRESS my heartfelt gratitude to those who lived out the stories in this book. I connected with almost all the individuals named in this book. To my delight, no one expressed an unwillingness to have a personal story included. Several were happy for me to use their real names. Even those who were not Christian were willing, and even pleased, to have their stories included. Hasan's response was typical of many. After he read the excerpt I sent, he said, "I am so happy to recall these events again. I have absolutely no objection to you using my story." Then he went on to tell me how he had recently listened to God regarding a work situation, heard God's voice, obeyed, and then saw how well the matter worked out.

One of the surprising joys of this project has been hearing the rest of the story when I asked for permission to include an account in this book. One couple related how they took their listening experience back to their team and then listened to God together. Rashid told me how he had been suicidal at the time of our listening experience, but six months later, he had a job. Patrick emailed me that he continued to think about the dream he shared with me. Jim told me God used the vision I saw when he was in my office to remind him he wanted to talk to me about something else.

I am grateful for Clinton, who spent many hours coaching me in listening to God. He also gave invaluable insight into each chapter as I wrote. This project would not have taken place without him.

I also want to thank an unnamed prophet at CTF Toronto. I stood in a long line of people, waiting to be prayed over. When he finally got to me, he put his finger on my chest and after a few encouraging words said, "Within you, in your heart, are books. You are going to write." I wondered if he had made a mistake. I certainly didn't expect that just over three years later, I would have written my first manuscript.

My parents have been instrumental in shaping me into the person I have become. My mother Helen, now with the Lord, wrote *The Hardest Place*, a biography of their former colleagues in Somalia. My father proofread a version of this manuscript and gave encouraging feedback. Long-term friends, such as Gus, Leonor, Peter, and many others, too numerous to mention, read early versions of this manuscript and encouraged me that the contents of this book were worth sharing.

I am deeply grateful for my wife, Ingrid. Thank you for sharing in my joy and encouraging me in this journey. Thank you for allowing me to go into writing mode and not talk for hours at a stretch. Thanks also for rounding up people for me to pray for.

Finally, I am deeply grateful to the Lord Jesus who makes this all possible. Jesus is the one who speaks to me and the one who assures me of his love for me.

Bibliography

Arnold, William T. "Vision(s)." In *Baker's Evangelical Dictionary of Biblical Theology*, by ed. Walter A. Elwell. Grand Rapids: Baker Book House, 1996. Accessed March 27, 2021. https://www.biblestudytools.com/dictionaries/bakers-evangelical-dictionary/visions.html.

Deere, Jack S. *Even in our Darkness: A Story of Beauty in a Broken Life*. Grand Rapids: Zondervan, 2018.

———. *Surprised by the Power of the Spirit: Discovering How God Speaks and Heals Today*. Grand Rapids: Zondervan, 1993

———. *Surprised by the Voice of God: How God Speaks Today Through Prophecies, Dreams, and Visions*. Grand Rapids: Zondervan, 1996.

Delitzsch, Franz. *A System of Biblical Psychology, Second English Edition*. Translated by Robert Ernest Wallis. Edinburgh: T. & T. Clark, 1866.

Eby, Richard E. *Caught Up Into Paradise*. Grand Rapids: Fleming H. Revell, 1990.

Epstein, David J. *Range: How Generalists Triumph in a Specialized World*. New York: Riverhead Books, 2019.

Fee, Gordon D., and Douglas Stuart. *How to Read the Bible for All Its Worth*. Grand Rapids: Zondervan, 1993.

Friesen, James G. et al. *Living From The Heart Jesus Gave You. 15th Anniversary Study Edition*. East Peoria, IL: Shepherd's House, Inc., 2016.

Geegh, Mary. *God Guides*. Holland, MI: Mission Partners India, 1900.

Got Questions Ministries. "What is Inductive Bible Study?" Accessed September 21, 2020. https://www.gotquestions.org/inductive-Bible-study.html.

Grudem, Wayne. *Systematic Theology: An Introduction to Biblical Doctrine*. Grand Rapids: Zondervan, 1994

Haye, Sophie de la. *Tread Upon the Lion: The Story of Tommie Titcombe*. Shoals, IN: Kingsley, 2013.

Healy, Blake K. *The Veil: An Invitation to the Unseen Realm*. Lake Mary, FL: Charisma House, 2018.

Huggett, Joyce. *Listening to God: Hearing His Voice. 30th Anniversary Edition*. London: Hodder & Stoughton, 2016.

Hurnard, Hannah. *Hearing Heart*. Carol Stream, IL: Tyndale House, 1981.

———. *Wayfarer in the Land*. Carol Stream, IL: Tyndale House, 1981.

Javed, Kinaan et al. *Neuroanatomy, Cerebral Cortex*. Treasure Island, FL: StatPearls, LLC, 2020. Accessed March 27, 2021. https://www.ncbi.nlm.nih.gov/books/NBK537247/?report=classic.

Jersak, Brad. *Can You Hear Me? Tuning in to the God Who Speaks*. Victoria: Trafford, 2003.

Joshua Project. Region: Asia, South. Frontier Ventures. 2021. Accessed April 30, 2021 https://joshuaproject.net/regions/4.

Kozub, Sophie. "Take a Deep Breath—No Really, It Will Calm Your Brain: A New Study Shows the Way You're Breathing Affects Your Mind." Vox Media. March 30, 2017. Accessed March 27, 2021. https://www.theverge.com/2017/3/30/15109762/deep-breath-study-breathing-affects-brain-neurons-emotional-state.

Kraft, Charles H. *Two Hours to Freedom: A Simple and Effective Model for Healing and Deliverance*. Grand Rapids, MI: Chosen Books, 2010.

Lehman, Karl. *The Immanuel Approach: For Emotional Healing and for Life*. Evanston, IL: Emmanuel, 2016.

Lowder, Stephanie. "The History of Mirror: Through A Glass, Darkly." Beinenstock Furniture Library, accessed December 31, 2020. https://www.furniturelibrary.com/mirror-glass-darkly.

Martin, Sara. "The Power of the Relaxation Response: A Behavioral Medicine Pioneer Reports on a Time-Tested Technique That Reverses Aging and Improves Health." Monitor, 32. October, 2008. Accessed March 27, 2021. https://www.apa.org/monitor/2008/10/relaxation.

Merriam-Webster.com Dictionary, s.v. "reconciliation," accessed March 18, 2021, https://www.merriam-webster.com/dictionary/reconciliation.

Mickelson's Enhanced Strong's Dictionaries of the Greek and Hebrew Testaments, 2nd ed. Kennesaw, Georgia: LivingSon, 2015.

Moran, Roy. *Spent Matches; Igniting the Signal Fire for the Spiritually Dissatisfied*. Nashville: Thomas Nelson, 2015.

Murray, Andrew. *The Indwelling Spirit*. Minneapolis: Bethany House, 2006.

Olesberg, Lindsay. "How to Do Inductive Bible Study." InterVarsity Collegiate Ministries. InterVarsity Christian Fellowship USA. October, 2016. Accessed December 31, 2020. https://collegiateministries.intervarsity.org/sites/collegiateministries/files/resource/file/How%20to%20Do%20Inductive%20Bible%20Study.pdf.

Plumptre, E. H. "The Book of the Prophet Jeremiah." In *An Old Testament Commentary for English Readers, Vol. V.* edited by Charles John Ellicot, 3–196. New York: Cassell & Company, Limited, 1884.

Rawlings, Maurice. *Beyond Death's Door*. Nashville: Thomas Nelson, 2008.

Riffel, Herman. *Dream Interpretation: A Biblical Understanding*. Shippensburg, PA: Destiny Image, 1993.

Rustenbach, Rusty. *Listening and Inner-Healing Prayer: Meeting God in the Broken Places*. Colorado Springs: NavPress, 2011.

Virkler, Mark and Patti. *4 Keys To Hearing God's Voice*. Shippensburg, PA: Destiny Image, 2010.

———. "Principles of Christian Dream Interpretation." Educating for Transformation. Edited by Donna Cox. 2004. Accessed December 31, 2020. https://revdonc.files.wordpress.com/2010/01/christian-dream-interpretation.pdf.

Vitrano, Deana Maryann. "Comparing Perception and Imagination at the Visual Cortex." Honors Thesis. Dickinson College. 2012. https://scholar.dickinson.edu/student_honors/12.

Vlymen, Michael Van. *How to See in the Spirit: A Practical Guide on Engaging the Spirit Realm*. Carmel, IN: Ministry Resources, 2013.

BIBLIOGRAPHY

Wardle, Terry. "Why Is the Past Always Present?" Healing Care Ministries. Accessed September 6, 2020. https://hcmi.kartra.com/videopage/whyisthepastalwayspresent.

Wikipedia, The Free Encyclopedia, s.v., "Dhikr," last modified April 17, 2021, https://en.wikipedia.org/wiki/Dhikr.

Wikipedia, The Free Encyclopedia, s.v., "Dream incubation," last modified December 20, 2020, https://en.wikipedia.org/wiki/Dream_incubation.

Wikipedia, The Free Encyclopedia, s.v., "South Asia," last modified April 28, 2021, https://en.wikipedia.org/wiki/South_Asia.

Willard, Dallas. *Hearing God: Developing a Conversational Relationship With God.* Downers Grove, IL: InterVarsity, 2012.

CPSIA information can be obtained
at www.ICGtesting.com
Printed in the USA
LVHW020719270423
744847LV00002B/9